THE FRANCISCAN
INTELLECTUAL TRADITION

TRACING ITS ORIGINS
AND
IDENTIFYING ITS CENTRAL
COMPONENTS

KENAN B. OSBORNE, O.F.M.

THE FRANCISCAN HERITAGE SERIES
VOLUME ONE

CFIT/ESC-OFM
2003

© The Franciscan Institute
St. Bonaventure University
St. Bonaventure, NY 14778
2003

**This pamphlet is the first in
The Franciscan Heritage Series
sponsored by the
Commission on the Franciscan Intellectual Tradition
of the English-speaking Conference of the
Order of Friars Minor
(CFIT/ESC-OFM)**

General Editor

Joseph P. Chinnici, O.F.M.

Assistant Editor

Elise Saggau, O.S.F.

ISBN
1-57659-200-6

Library of Congress Control Number
2003103891

Printed and bound in the United States of America
BookMasters, Inc.
Mansfield, Ohio

TABLE OF CONTENTS

Table of Contents

GENERAL EDITOR'S INTRODUCTION

On behalf of the Commission for the Retrieval of the Franciscan Intellectual Tradition (CFIT), I present to you with great pleasure this first volume of The Franciscan Heritage Series—*The Franciscan Intellectual Tradition: Tracing Its Origins and Identifying Its Central Components* by Kenan B. Osborne, O.F.M. The purpose of this first volume is to present some general and major themes of the theological formulation of the Franciscan Intellectual Tradition as these themes intersect with contemporary perspectives. It provides both a fine starting point for further reflection and a solid foundation for future expositions in this series.

Dr. Osborne, a member of the Order of Friars Minor, Province of Saint Barbara, and Emeritus Professor at the Franciscan School of Theology, Berkeley, California, is an internationally recognized theologian who specializes in sacramental theology, Christology, ecclesiology and the multicultural dimensions of Christian theology. He has here presented in brief form an excellent introduction. It is our hope that readers will take this short work and, with careful and thoughtful study, perhaps under the guidance of a mentor, begin to plumb the spiritual depths of our inheritance and comprehend the important uniqueness of its intellectual expression. Through reflection, prayer, conversation and action may we also explore these theological themes as they might be expressed in preaching, pastoral practice, the works of evangelization and community formation with friars, sisters and laity.

This present work takes its place within the context of a much larger Franciscan Heritage Series, which we hope will encompass topics such as Creation, the Iconography of the Crucified, Christian Anthropology, Ecclesiology, Scriptural Themes, Evangelization, History, the Natural Sciences, the Arts and other areas of contemporary concern. As the volumes develop, we hope also to include some of the many different carriers of our Franciscan Tradition—not just Francis and the cleric theologians, but also Clare, the women penitents and the laity.

Before our readers begin to taste the "first fruit" of a large and expansive feast, however, we must briefly indicate, in this

Introduction, the origins of the Heritage Series, its relationship to a major initiative in the English-speaking world, and its connections with some significant trajectories in the social and ecclesial experience of the brothers and sisters of the thirteenth-century foundational period of the Franciscan family.

The Franciscan Intellectual Tradition Project

In March 2001, the English-speaking Conference, Order of Friars Minor, undertook an initiative for the contemporary retrieval of the Franciscan Intellectual Tradition. Composed of the leaders of the provinces and other entities of England, Ireland, Canada and the United States, the Conference established an inter-obediential commission to facilitate the coordination and networking of various publications and popular initiatives that were already taking place throughout the English-speaking world in the various countries which were represented. As one its first initiatives, this Commission for the Retrieval of the Franciscan Intellectual Tradition (CFIT) composed and published a strategic five-year plan, the purpose of which was sevenfold:

- To identify the major themes of the Franciscan Intellectual Tradition;

- To provide training programs and resources for formators and those called to serve in leadership with respect to the nature and unique contributions of the Franciscan Intellectual Tradition;

- To network and foster collaboration among the current Franciscan study centers of the English-speaking world: The Franciscan Institute and School of Franciscan Studies, St. Bonaventure, New York; the Franciscan School of Theology, Berkeley, California; the Franciscan Study Center, Canterbury, England; and two major theological schools with a Franciscan presence, the Catholic Theological Union in Chicago and the Washington Theological Union in Washington, DC.

- To promote and support the broader and wider articulation and communication of the Franciscan Intellectual Tradition with respect to our evangelizing mission;

- To identify and encourage new scholars, especially among the laity;

- To create new learning opportunities as might be needed, for example, through the establishment of a website and the possibility of distance learning;

- To make a greater and more conscious effort to provide leadership training and resources to Franciscans throughout the English-speaking world.

The Commission decided very early that one of its first major tasks would be to identify the central themes and emphases of the Franciscan Intellectual Tradition, particularly as these were embodied in key theological issues. We decided to begin on the theological level since we felt that the tradition first took on its specific contours in this area and that theological reflection might provide the clearest orientation for our contemporary mission in Church and society. The Commission also recognized, however, that the Franciscan Intellectual Tradition is rich in insights as to how the Christian message might intersect with the fields of politics, economics, psychology, sociology and environmental studies. Its own work would simply be complementing many other initiatives being undertaken in the wider Franciscan family, for example, among the many colleges and universities working to mainstream their inherited Franciscan charism.

After an initial overview statement that was published along with the Strategic Plan in a booklet entitled *The Franciscan Intellectual Tradition Project* (June, 2001, available from the Franciscan Institute, St. Bonaventure, New York), two significant initiatives were immediately undertaken. The first was the publication of the proceedings of the annual forum on Franciscan theology at the Washington Theological Union. This gathering is designed to interface, at a high scholarly level, the major theological themes of the Tradition with contemporary issues. Two publications represent the first efforts to make these insightful reflections available: *The Franciscan Intellectual Tradition* (St. Bonaventure, NY: The Franciscan Institute,

2002); *Franciscan Identity and Postmodern Culture* (St. Bonaventure, NY: The Franciscan Institute, 2003). Subsequent volumes of symposia papers will address Creation, the Church, and Biblical Foundations.

The development and publication of a series of pamphlets entitled The Franciscan Heritage Series is the second major initiative. This Series has a different audience in mind and is pitched at a level different from the Washington Theological Union symposia essays. The Heritage Series is designed to make available to college teachers, preachers, formation directors, pastoral workers, and lay persons associated with the Franciscan movement some of the basic themes dominant in our Intellectual Tradition. The character of these offerings is less academic. While they presuppose some training in philosophy and theology, they try, as much as possible, to keep scholarly references to a minimum and to avoid the technical language associated with medieval scholasticism. Although each is complete in itself, no one volume is fully expository. In the long run, we hope that the compilation of multiple volumes will enable the lively student to grasp the Franciscan Intellectual Tradition in its totality.

The First Volume

In this context, the purpose of the first volume in the Series is fourfold :

(1) To situate the Franciscan Intellectual Tradition within the broader sweep of the Church's own Scriptural and Magisterial Theological Tradition;

(2) To identify some of the major themes in the Franciscan spiritual-theological vision of Catholic Christian life;

(3) To give an overview of our Tradition's specific development and its major writers;

(4) To present readers with enough background in the categories in which our academic theological tradition was first articulated (i.e. the philosophy of Aristotle) so that they might be both somewhat attuned to the reading of the primary texts of the thirteenth century and somewhat prepared to translate the major themes into the

philosophical, psychological and sociological categories of our own day. This first volume is thus foundational for those that will follow.

We recognize that readers of any given pamphlet may find some of its insights either too difficult to grasp or perhaps too generalized; hopefully some insights will be stimulating and encouraging. We anticipate that the volumes themselves might prove most helpful in classrooms, discussion groups and formation settings. We hope that readers might translate the basic themes presented in The Franciscan Heritage Series into still more popular forms and make them accessible to an ever-wider public of interested parties. We would like to sponsor two-page summaries and updates, in printed and web-page format, which might help form preaching, meditation and community conversation, and serve as an even more practical illustration of basic principles. Each person and each "community of learning" has a different role to play in the larger project. May the Lord, in an ever-deeper fashion, show each of us a way to make these profound insights and truths life-giving in our Church and society. Dr. Osborne has here given us a fine start.

Making Connections

Many people associated with the Franciscan family live on a very practical and pastoral level. We are called to engage our neighbor in following the footprints of Our Lord and the way of Francis and Clare. The vision, after all, begins with an encounter with a leper and the making of mercy; in its very simplicity it reveals the "sweetness of God." We may find intellectual formulations, particularly of an academic nature, abstract and removed from everyday concerns, lacking in application. Our Franciscan tradition, as it has developed over the centuries, has tended to separate the insights of spirituality from the insights of academic theology, the inspiration and intuition of Francis from the institutional work of Bonaventure and the philosophical-theological vision of Scotus, the formation experience of novitiate from the school experience of preparation for ministry. We believe that these are lamentable divisions, ones that need particular healing in this contemporary era. We want our Franciscan life to be whole—a comprehensive way of looking at the world that can animate our acting, our feeling and our thinking

On the one hand, we readily recognize the fellow members of our family whenever we gather together. In some fashion, at a very profound and intuitive level, a common heart has shaped our life's endeavors. On the other hand, when we gather together, we also search for a common public language, in both thought and practice, which can express our deepest communal bonds. We struggle to share our Gospel experience among ourselves and with others, to formulate it in common ritual, to embody it in shared institutions and to communicate it in a communal "thought style." When others ask us "What does it mean to be Franciscan?" we can easily *show* them. Can we also accompany our *showing* with a *telling* and thus *enable an action, an understanding and a bonding communication*?

We would also wish for a unity of vision and practice to be established between our brothers and sisters engaged in social work, institutional administration, education and individual ministries. Our social locations are different, but are we that far apart? We would want the same gospel charism and intuition to reach both the marginated and the more powerful, so that all might see themselves as members of one family, brothers and sisters of one another. Today, at this time in the Church's history and in the social, cultural and political climate of the twenty-first century, we would wish to present a vision that can encourage and unite all of God's creatures. Such is the hope of the CFIT. Our Franciscan Heritage Series is a small attempt to help bridge some gaps between our Franciscan experience of life and our intellectual formulations, between our personal longings and our public languages, between our spirituality and our theology.

We note, in this first volume, the strong link between the spirituality and vision of Francis of Assisi, sometimes referred to as his "vernacular theology," and the academic expression of this theology in the early schools at Paris and Oxford. The connection exists at a very profound level, and perhaps it will help readers to envision the unity that the CFIT is trying to foster as emerging from the intersection between

1. the challenges that Francis faced in the Church and society of his time, his social location;

2. his own gospel experience as elucidated in his *Testament* in response to the social and ecclesial challenges;

3. the different languages in which this has been commu-
    nicated over time.

Let us briefly consider each of these.

1. The *challenges of social location* faced by Francis of Assisi are in
many ways similar to our own. Simply put, he was born into a world
that, in some respects, had forgotten what it means to be both human and Christian. Confronted with a new awareness of the presence of the poor in its own society, medieval Italy developed rituals
of exclusion to protect itself both economically and culturally from
the threatening presence of the other, symbolically identified as
"leper" or "heretic" or "criminal" or "infidel" or, from the perspective of the underside, "the priest" or "the powerful."

There was a distinct effort to bridge the gap between the strong
and the weak, the possessors and the dispossessed, those who be-
longed and those who needed to be expelled. This effort became
ever more difficult as society itself experienced civil strife and a
struggle for a dominating power that could establish a peaceful public order. Alienation caused by the complicity of the Church in inherited social structures and the search to reclaim the gospel message occasioned an explosion of popular movements, a papal and
episcopal desire for ecclesial reform, the development of marginal
groups, the acceptance by some of a division between spirituality
and religion, between institutional rituals and personal ways of salvation. In the larger world, people were torn between two compet-
ing allegiances, the Church and the Empire, and between two reli-
gions confronting each other for global dominance, the Christians
and the Saracens. In the world that Francis inherited, people posed
very direct questions related to *human suffering, human belonging, human peace, human integrity, human transformation* and, ultimately, the
goodness of God and the *goodness of being human.*

2. Into this world, not away from it, the Lord led Francis of Assisi
to do penance, to work and to discover "sweetness." And thus the jour-
ney has been for succeeding generations of Franciscans. Francis en-
countered God in the condition of being human, in a condition that
was most disfigured, in a condition of exclusion and poverty, in the
condition of God-with-us, Emmanuel, in the condition of a disfig-

ured but grace-filled Church, in the human condition of the "infi-del." He began to work with his hands, as did his Master, to become "simple and subject to all" (Francis, *Testament* 19), to imitate as a co-worker a Creator who made all things, redeemed all things and would bring all things to their transformation (cf. Francis, *Earlier Rule* 23). He began to take up the cross of his own body, which came with a human condition embedded in a disfigured world. In doing this, Francis was called to follow the path of the Incarnate Lord, who did not disdain to be born, labor along the way and die.

From this One, Francis drew life. Francis grew in this God-with-us reality to experience all things in relationship, to develop a praxis of fraternity and peace, to become a universal brother to brothers and sisters and to all creatures. He began to be not repelled by this condition of being human but inspired by its beauty, its goodness, its creative power, its dependency on the Creator. He began to see the presence of the Lord shining through the face of the world. Here was his gospel answer to the world's challenges and his gospel "yes" to the condition of being human. His was a way of *love-willing-to-suffer*, a way of *belonging, peace, integrity, transformation*, and a proc-lamation of *goodness at the heart of reality*.

3. With the help of others, Francis found a *language* to express this intuition about God-with-us in his prayers, his creed, his ser-mons, his letters, his Rule, his evangelizing work and preaching, and his symbolic texts of Crib, Cross and Eucharist. He left also for others the human and graced text of his own life. Those who fol-lowed after the first brothers inherited this intuition, received these texts and the symbolic text of Francis's own stigmata, confronted the problems of their times, and, in different languages (ones both shaped by their own milieux, their own possibilities, and constrained by their own communal disfigurements), still tried to express this great vision of God-with-us.

The same questions needed to be answered, albeit from a differ-ent social location—questions of *human suffering, human belonging, human peace, human integrity, human transformation*, and ultimately, *the goodness of God* and *the goodness of being human*. The same world needed anew the gospel music of "yes" and the following of the one who became human, labored and died for us. And herein lay a basic continuity between Francis, Clare, Thomas of Celano, the Three

Companions, John of Perugia, Angela of Foligno, Elizabeth of Hungary, Bonaventure, Peter John Olivi, Scotus and so many other brothers and sisters. In the Franciscan Intellectual Tradition we find again and again, in different languages using different genres, the same fundamentals of our vision of the Catholic Christian life. Dr. Osborne has given us in this first pamphlet a few indicators:

- **God's presence and universal accessibility in Christ—** in creation, in the poor, in the non-event, in the non-believer;

- **God as a community of persons, a Trinity, sharing life and goods**—a model for fraternity, social peace, relationality, mission and the exchange of goods between peoples;

- **God's gratuity and liberality to be with us, even in our creaturely disfigured way**—in Christ's birth, life and passion, in each unique creature, in the great gift of the Church with its people and priests and theologians and sacraments and doctrine and teaching magisterium;

- **God's human way of exercising authority, creating order and "being with"**—through example, humility, courtesy, respect and love-willing-to-suffer with the neighbor.

Embedded in this vision and communicated in this Franciscan Intellectual Tradition are implications for the world of politics, economics, social relations, family life and daily human existence. Can we speak in the midst of our own social and ecclesial location a language of God-with-us, a language of life, a language of ritual, a language of social witness, a language of the intellect that, for our own time, will have us "do what is ours to do" in this Christian Catholic Franciscan way of gospel life? Such is the CFIT's purpose and hope in seeking companions on the way. May the reader beware!

Joseph P. Chinnici, OFM
Franciscan School of Theology
Berkeley, California 94709
March 19, 2003

PART ONE
INTRODUCTORY REMARKS

The Franciscan Intellectual Tradition is a philosophical and theological expression of understanding the Catholic faith. As a philosophy and theology, this tradition is one of several major interpretations of this faith. In the history of the western Catholic Church, two other major traditions have enriched the Catholic faith: the Dominican Intellectual Tradition, centered on the writings of St. Thomas Aquinas, and the Augustinian Intellectual Tradition, centered on the writings of St. Augustine of Hippo. All three traditions have continually received the blessing of popes and scholars. They have also intersected with each other, have influenced each other and have been self-consciously aware of their differences. None of them, however, can claim to be the "better" intellectual tradition. Since they are philosophical and theological interpretations of the Catholic Faith, all three respect the fundamental teachings of Scripture, Tradition and the magisterium.

The focus in the volumes of this series is on the Franciscan Intellectual Tradition, but references to the other two major traditions will, at times, be necessary. The primary sources for the differences held by the Franciscan tradition stem from the distinctive spiritual experience and vision of Francis and Clare of Assisi. Francis and Clare were not theologians, in the academic interpretation of this word, but they both attempted, in their lives and in their writings, to speak and to exemplify the Word of God. By their way of life, they wanted to deepen their own Catholic faith and share gospel holiness with the people they met. Their voices echoed the gospels and Catholic tradition in a new and convincing way. Their spiritual vision became enormously attractive, and many men and women joined their communities.

It is estimated that by the year 1221, about eleven years after St. Francis formed a small group of followers, the number of Franciscan friars ranged from three thousand to five thousand. This was a phenomenal growth. In addition, after the first Franciscan students began to attend the major universities in Europe around 1219, their Franciscan spirituality impressed several key diocesan professors of theology, particularly at the uni-

versities of Paris and Oxford. Theological insights gradually inter-
faced with the distinctive Franciscan spirituality, and this development became what we today call the Franciscan Intellectual Tradition.

Theology is never the same as dogma or the solemn teachings of
the Church. Theology is a continual reflection on faith; it presup-
poses faith; it is not in competition with faith. However, from the
Pauline letters onwards, one finds a number of such reflections on
Catholic faith, each specifically differing both in philosophical approaches and in theological approaches. It is true that in the contemporary Catholic Church, Thomism is the more popular theological approach among Catholic writers, but popularity by itself never
creates definitive doctrine.

In the history of the Western Catholic Church, the Augustinian
Intellectual Tradition extended its own overarching popularity from
400 C.E. to 1300 C.E. Even after 1300, this Tradition remained very
influential. In the sixteenth century, both Martin Luther and John
Calvin employed citations from the writings of St. Augustine second only in number to their citations from the Scriptures. Catholic
theologians at the Council of Trent were also very competent in their
knowledge of the Augustinian Intellectual Tradition, since the Council of Trent was in many ways an "Augustinian" council. Bishops
and theologians were arguing against the "Augustinian" approach
of the major reformers. The Catholic bishops and theologians at Trent
were also trained in the Dominican and Franciscan intellectual traditions and these positions are also evident in the council documents.

At the end of the thirteenth century and the beginning of the
fourteenth century, the Dominican Friars formally selected the teachings of Thomas Aquinas as the center of their theological formation.
This formal move guaranteed a long life for the Dominican Intellectual Tradition. The Franciscans followed this pattern by selecting
both Bonaventure and John Duns Scotus as the center of their Intellectual Tradition. From 1300 C.E. to 1563 C.E. (the conclusion of the
Council of Trent), the intellectual traditions of the two mendicant
orders became far more popular than the Augustinian Tradition.
During this same period of time, the two mendicant traditions became competitive with each other, and at the Council of Trent, the
numbers of bishops and their theologians were almost divided in
half—one half leaning to the Dominican tradition and the other half

to the Franciscan. After the Council of Trent, the Franciscan Intellectual Tradition slowly lost its dominance. However, among Franciscans themselves, this tradition was kept very much alive.

Theological writings, in all three of these traditions, were in Latin. There were two clear foundations—God and Jesus. The first foundation, the Triune God, was very often discussed intellectually in writings called *De Deo Uno et Trino*. This is often translated in English as *The Theology of the One and Triune God*. The second foundation, the Word made flesh, was dealt with in writings most often called *De Verbo Incarnato*. In English, an abbreviated translation of this Latin phrase is "christology," and "christology" has become the term most often used by theologians for presentations on Jesus. In this volume, I will use the terms "Triune God" and "christology" as designations of the longer phrases—the theology of the "One and Triune God" and the theology of the "Word made flesh."

All three of the major intellectual traditions in the Western Church—the Augustinian Tradition, the Dominican Tradition and the Franciscan Tradition—are based on the same sources for these two foundations, namely, Scripture, Tradition and magisterial teaching. None of these intellectual traditions, however, started as a creation from nothing. All three inherited philosophical theologies of the past on which they continued to build. In other words, the basis for all three is identical, namely, the revealed Word of God as expressed in Scripture, Tradition and the solemn teachings of the Church. Differences are based on the various philosophical and theological ways in which the three intellectual traditions express the implications of the revealed Word of God and on the interfacing of spirituality and theology, an interfacing that is most evident in the Franciscan Intellectual Tradition.

In the Roman Catholic Church, there has never been a single christology; hence the better term is plural: "christologies." Nor has there been a single theology of the Triune God; hence the better term is plural: "theologies of God/Trinity." Each theology of the Triune God and each christology has been *developed* through a lengthy *process*. Over time, some of these theologies and christologies have become non-relevant. Others are still operative today. Most of those still operative continue to remain in process, since they are being further developed and more carefully honed by contemporary theologians. If one includes the Eastern churches in this overview, the extent of the differences in these theologies of God and christologies becomes even more dramatic, since the several Eastern theologies on the Trinity and on Jesus are quite diverse. The theologies of the Eastern churches are based on the same three foundations as in the West—holy Scripture, holy Tradition and holy Doctrine.

Over the past two thousand years, the world has never experienced a theological "golden age," that is, an age by which all subsequent theological ages are to be judged. This means that there is in the Roman Catholic Church no "one theology" or "one christology"that is definitive. Rather, there are and have been many theologies and christologies, all of which are based on the same foundation of God's revealed Word. To understand and to live the Word of God, revealed in both creation and incarnation, has been and will be a continuing task for Christians. The schools of theology that developed in the thirteenth century must be seen against this background. The scholars we will examine intended to express the Word of God, revealed in both creation and incarnation, in such a way that the people of their time might understand and incorporate into the depths of their spiritual lives this saving Word. To some extent, the present series on the Franciscan Intellectual Tradition is an attempt to perform the same task for the twenty-first century, with its peculiar challenges and opportunities.

The three major intellectual traditions are philosophical and theological interpretations of Western Catholic Faith. The following material, therefore, must be seen as a description, in widebrush strokes, of theological developments with special emphasis on the Western not Eastern Catholic Church. Because it is merely an overview or outline, it is necessarily generalized. Its purpose is to indicate the development of Catholic theologies, which are fundamentally based on two foundations of Christian belief, namely, on God, who is one and triune, and on Jesus, the Word made flesh. In what follows, the time periods are rough generalities. They include significant events in the West that strongly modified the efforts of theologians in forming both christological and trinitarian thought.

PART TWO
HISTORICAL OVERVIEW
30 C.E. TO 1300 C.E.

The First Period: 30 C.E. to 70 C.E.

This period begins with the Resurrection/Pentecost event and ends with the destruction of the Second Temple in Jerusalem. After the Resurrection, the disciples spoke about Jesus, retelling things he had said and done. They also shared their feelings and their perceptions of the Jesus-event in their lives, perhaps not so much through theological language as through the language of spirituality. God and Jesus were the centers of their faith. These early followers of Jesus prayed together at special times, but they also continued to attend the synagogue and temple services. As practicing and pious Jews, they explained how Jesus was the fulfillment of the Torah, the Prophets and the Writings. For all Jews at that time, these texts were reverenced as the sacred books. Through Moses, through the prophets and through Jewish leaders, God's love, God's covenant and God's commandments were revealed.

At times, these early followers of Jesus found that some of the sacred writings did not seem to have Jesus as their fulfillment. At other times, connections were easily made. From 30 to 70, the Jesus community struggled to piece together the meaning of Jesus' life and teaching, his death and resurrection with their Jewish belief in the God of the covenant. The writings of St. Paul indicate this in a striking way. Paul was a well-trained Jewish scholar, perhaps a rabbi but certainly a Pharisee, who in a dramatic way went from persecuting the followers of Jesus to becoming one of Jesus' most important followers. In his letters we see a learned Jew struggling to integrate the Torah, the Prophets and the Writings into the Jesus event. The Jewish God, Yahweh, and the Jewish Jesus, in whom God's covenant with the Jews reached its fulfillment, are the two poles that unite the teaching, preaching and prayer life of Paul and all other early followers of Jesus.

These early followers considered themselves Jewish. They did not identify themselves as "Christian." They called themselves "brethren" (Acts 1:16), disciples (Acts 11:26), and "those of the way" (Acts, 9:2; 22:4; 24:14). They did not believe that they were part of a new religion, founded to be distinct from Judaism. Many of them continued to follow Jewish religious practices. Nor did they see themselves as a "Christian church." Their self-identity was Jewish. Other Jews considered them as one of the many "Judaisms" or Jewish sects, which were quite active at that time. The Book of Acts (11:26 and 26:28) does make mention of "Christian" as a name others had begun applying to the followers of Jesus. Some scholars place the first, tenuous use of this designation at Antioch in Syria about 40 C.E., but not all biblical scholars accept this early date. Actually, it is not until late in the first century that the word "Christian" became a general designation for the followers of Jesus as a group distinct from the Jews. The *Annals* of Tacitus (15:44), written about 64 C.E., refer to the followers of Jesus as Christians. The designation "Christian" is also found in 1 Pet. 4:16, in Trajan's letter to the emperor in 112 C.E., and in Pliny the Younger's (61 C.E.-113 C.E.) letter to Trajan (*Epistola* 10:96).

The caution about the use of the term "Christian" during the period 30-70 C.E. is important for the following reason: current New Testament scholarship stresses that the self-identity of the followers of Jesus was actually Jewish. Only when the followers of Jesus were either thrown out of the synagogue or membership became predominantly non-Jewish does the term "Christian" begin to describe their self-identity as distinct from Judaism. Although many scholars continue to use the term "Christian" for the early followers of Jesus from the time of the Resurrection to the destruction of the Temple, this usage leads readers to regard the followers of Jesus as a group quite distinct from the Jewish people of that time. It implies that these early followers of Jesus already had a clear "Christian self-identity" and that the meaning of the term is similar if not the same as the meaning in our own contemporary understanding. However, what we mean by "Christian" today cannot be simply predicated of Jesus' early followers. "Christian" implies today many issues and determinations which were simply unthinkable at that time.

During this period (30-70), there apparently were some written materials on Jesus, e.g., the Q source, the proto-Mark, accounts of

Jesus' arrest and death and accounts about his Resurrection. We have no manuscripts of these writings. We have only reflections of them in the four gospels, and these reflections cannot be seen as word-for-word citations. The gospel writers adapted the original wording to fit their respective needs. The authentic Pauline letters were written during this same period, and they contain much about the meaning of Jesus but only a few details of his life. From 30 C.E. to 70 C.E., then, we have only inchoative theologies on Jesus and his relationship to the One God.

The Second Period: 70 C.E. to 100 C.E.

From 70 C.E. to 100 C.E., a large part of the New Testament was written—the four gospels, the Acts of the Apostles, the pastoral letters and the book of Revelation, all of which give us written beginnings of christology and, to some degree, of the theology of the Trinity. The Synoptic Gospels and Acts were written earlier in this period and the Johannine Gospel and Johannine Letters towards the end, as also some of the Pseudo-Pauline Letters, the book of Revelation, and the letters of James, Peter and Jude. In these writings there is no "one christology" or "one theology" that explains how the humanity of Jesus is united to the One God. There are, however, foundational beginnings of several christologies.

Basically, all the material in the four gospels is a reflection by an author (Mark, Matthew, Luke, John), and probably these reflections on Jesus and God also express an understanding of Jesus in their respective communities. The evangelists are authors in their own right, but they are also spokesmen and teachers in local communities. During this period, here and there and little by little, the process of separation from post-temple Judaism began to take place. By 120 C.E. there was a Christian self-consciousness among the followers of Jesus, but at the same time this Christian self-consciousness included the self-identity of the followers of Jesus as the "true Israel." In other words, their identity was Christian *and* Jewish. It was Christian because of their acceptance of Jesus as Messiah and their belief in the close unity of Jesus and Yahweh. One might say that they believed in "Yahweh-Jesus." It was also Jewish, since in spite of their separation from the Jewish people, the followers of Jesus claimed as their own the Torah, the Covenant, the Prophets, the name

Israel and the title "God's chosen people." In other words, they claimed what was essential to Judaism, believing that all had been fulfilled in Jesus. The followers of Jesus were the "new Israel," and they had a "new covenant," which cancelled the old covenant. This position is very evident in the early apologetic writings.

Both the growing number of non-Jews in the Jesus communities and the antagonism of some Jewish groups (e.g., the rabbis at Jamnia) played major roles in the process of separation. As the process of self-identification developed, the "Christian-Jewish" followers of Jesus began to be regarded as belonging to a distinct "religion." As the Greek influence became more prominent, they gradually saw themselves as a new religion, namely, Christian—a Christian church with a Christian faith. To place such a developed identity into the years prior to 90-100 C.E., however, leads to a misreading of New Testament texts.

The Third Period: 100 C.E. to 325 C.E.

This period extends roughly from the time of the earliest theologians and Fathers of the Church down to the first council of the Church at Nicaea in 325 C.E. During this time Christian theologians began to develop a more systematic presentation of christology and a more detailed trinitarian theology. However, in this period, there are several christologies and trinitarian theologies and not simply "one form" of a philosophico-theological system. Theologians of this period include: Ignatius of Antioch, Justin of Rome, Clement of Alexandria, Melito of Sardis, Irenaeus of Lyon, Origen of Alexandria, Tertullian of Carthage and Paul of Samosata. There were also other minor theologians. The unorthodox theological and christological views of Arius of Alexandria were especially important in the years just prior to the Council of Nicaea.

Prominent movements of various scholars and their followers also developed. These movements often brought about great disharmony among Christian churches simply because of the large number of Christian followers of such movements. There was one primary issue in all of them—How can Jesus be at one and the same time a human being and also God? Some authors presented Jesus as the Messiah or as the prophet who was to come just before the end of the world. This way of presenting Jesus did not offer any major theological problem, for Jesus was accepted as the Messiah foretold in the Old Testament. However, the idea of an incarnation, i.e., God becoming human, quickly became the major issue that galvanized this entire period. It was the focus of both christological and trinitarian thinking. It produced a flurry of explanations that were quite diverse. Some were considered acceptable and some not acceptable. The issue of acceptability or non-acceptability became a further complicating factor—who had the competence to judge one view as acceptable and another as not acceptable? There was, in this early period, no monolithic understanding of who could make authoritative judgments.

During this same period (100-325), the theology of redemption or salvation did not receive the same attention as the christological/ trinitarian focus. In fact, there were only small beginnings of a theology of redemption. There was no clear theology of church, often called "ecclesiology," and no clear theology of the sacraments. The early theological formulations of christological and trinitarian belief were developed more or less on their own, that is, with no influence from a theology of church or of redemption. Today, all these theologies, that is, christology, trinitiarian theology, theology of church, theology of redemption and theology of sacraments, interface with one another. What theologians present in their discussions of christology or trinity has major implications for a theology of church, redemption and sacraments. The opposite is also true—what one says theologically about church, redemption and sacraments has major implications for both christology and trinitarian theology. Because of this inter-connection, there has always been a developing aspect of theology.

During this early period, there were many divisions, some small and some large. Not only were there clashing theological positions, but also there were clashing political positions. Different languages (Hebrew, Aramaic, Syriac, Greek, Latin, etc.) complicated communication. Key words were often interpreted differently when translations were made. All of this contributed to major discussions, arguments, debates and disagreements about the meaning of Jesus and the meaning of the relationship between the human Jesus and the Logos. Nor was this simply a discussion among theologically trained individuals. These issues were discussed by ordinary Christians in the market place and in restaurants. Rarely does theology have such a wide venue of discussion.

The Fourth Period: The Councils of the Early Church—325 C.E. to 681 C.E.

This period includes the following: the first Council of Nicaea (325 C.E.), the first Council of Constantinople (381 C.E.), the Council of Ephesus (431 C.E.), the Council of Chalcedon (451 C.E.), the second Council of Constantinople (553 C.E.) and the third Council of Constantinople (681 C.E.). It was during the preparation, the sessions and the immediate aftermath of these councils that the christological faith of the Christian Church became clarified. After the Council of Chalcedon, there were some further clarifications made at the second and third Councils of Constantinople, (rejection of Nestorianism, monophysitism, monothelitism and monenergism). *Since these councils, no other council of the Church has made any further solemn christological declaration.* Doctrinal development of christological issues stopped at this point. Subsequent Church councils have simply restated the positions developed by these four councils. The Second Vatican Council focused on ecclesiology. Its christological stance can only be inferred from the explicit ecclesiology described in the conciliar documents. There is no indication that the bishops at Vatican II had a form of christology that was different from the Logos-christology of the first four councils.

As the early Fathers and theologians of the Church tried to clarify the meaning of the incarnation, they also kept rethinking their understanding of God as relational. The very reality of God, they argued, must be seen as relational, if the Christian community believes that the Logos became incarnate in the human nature of Jesus. Slowly but surely, these early Christian thinkers began to develop a theology of God in which the emphasis was not on a singularly transcendent God, but on a relationally transcendent God. They began to envision God not as singularly immanent, but as relationally immanent. Historically, it was this theological struggle to understand that Jesus is God (incarnation) that gave rise to a theology of a relational God (the Trinity). Whenever one speaks about a Trinitarian God, it is necessary to recall the intrinsic connection between the theology of Trinity and the theology of incarnation. During this period, Athanasius (+373), Cyril of Alexandria (375-444) and the bishops at the Council of Chalcedon (451) built on the previous thought of Irenaeus and Origen. They pushed for an understanding of a relational God. Basil the Great (+379), Gregory of Nyssa (335-395), Gregory of Nazianz (329-390), Evagrius of Pontus (344-399), Augustine (354-430), Maximus the Confessor (580-622) and Dionysius the Areopagite (sixth century) all contributed in various ways to a vision that is at one and the same time cosmic and christocentric, unifying all creation in a loving communion.

The Fifth Period: The Development of Scholastic Theology—1000 C.E. to 1300 C.E.

In this period, the Augustinian Intellectual Tradition was renewed and the Franciscan and Dominican Intellectual Traditions, building on the insights of Holy Scripture and the great Fathers of the Church, each in its own way formulated a summa—a gathering of rich theological traditions, influenced in various ways by Aristotelian philosophy. From 1000 C.E. to the end of 1200 C.E., a number of intellectual issues combined to form what scholars have called "scholasticism." Three key components of scholasticism and its method can be identified—the Dialectical Method, the Aristotelian Philosophical Texts, and the Four Books of Sentences.

1. **The Dialectical Method**. In the twelfth century the dialectical method became widespread in the various centers of theological teaching (monastic schools and cathedral schools). In some form or other, this method used differing statements taken from the Fathers of the Church, early medieval theologians, and even popes and bishops. It juxtaposed positions on particular issues, presenting those that favored the position (*sic*, "yes") and those that opposed the position (*non*, "no"). It then arrived at a conclusion. This method, called "sic et non," became standard for teaching theology at the medieval universities.

2. **Aristotelian Philosophical Texts**. Aristotle's writings had been translated from Greek into Latin by the Islamic scholars, Avicenna (980-1037) and Averroës (1126-1198). These two scholars also wrote Latin commentaries on sections of Aristotelian thought. From the time of Augustine (himself included), few Western theologians, scholars and writers were fluent in Greek or even knew any Greek. Since Avicenna and Averroës were the first to render Aristotle into Latin, their

works provided the first opportunity for medieval Western scholars to have any first-hand access to Aristotelian philosophy. From the time of the early Fathers, especially St. Augustine, down to the eleventh and twelfth centuries, Platonic philosophy had dominated Western Catholic thought. Gradually, from 1000 to 1300, a change to Aristotelian philosophy took place in the Western Church. Medieval theologies both of God and of Jesus were developed using Aristotelian philosophical positions, at least in some ways. Most often, these theological developments employed both Platonic and Aristotelian elements of philosophy.

3. The Four Books of Sentences. Peter Lombard (c. 1100-1160) composed a theological text called *The Sentences*. This volume was divided into four books. Book One examined the Trinity; Book Two considered creation, grace and sin; Book Three centered on the incarnation, redemption and virtue; and Book Four dealt with the sacraments and eschatology. From the early thirteenth century to the mid-seventeenth century, this work became "the text" for theology, second only to the Bible.

In a short time, Western Catholic theological study developed a *common method*, a *common philosophy* and a *common text* for all the universities and schools where theology was taught. Lectures, formal discussions (i.e., *quaestiones disputatae*) and written commentaries on the *Sentences* by all the Masters (*Magistri*) of theology were basically unified. Thus, in the thirteenth century, the renewed Augustinian Intellectual Tradition and the newly formulated Dominican and Franciscan Intellectual Traditions shared a basic similarity in method, in philosophical framework and in lectures and commentaries on the same textual material. An understanding of the different theological positions and the emphases of each tradition must begin with understanding this method, this philosophical framework, and this textbook. Major theologians within these traditions basically accepted to some degree the philosophical framework of Aristotle, but these same scholars subsequently used the Aristotelian framework in differing ways. They each, in very distinct ways, connected Aristotelian thought to the following five theological issues:

1. **The relationship of God to creation.** Is the image and vestige of God in creation an image and vestige of the Trinity or of the One God? Is the image and vestige of God in creation due to God's goodness, i.e., God as the fountain of goodness (*Fons bonitatis*), or to God's omnipotence or to God's knowledge?

2. **The relationship of creation to incarnation.** Is the incarnation basically a redemptive or salvific gift of God to a sinful creation, or is the incarnation the very reason for creation, with human sin no longer in a central place?

3. **The relationship of creation, incarnation and final risen life in God.** Is the incarnation a unique moment or a unique event, or is there an incarnational presence in creation itself and an incarnational presence in risen life?

4. **The relationship of God's freedom to creation, incarnation and risen life.** Is God's freedom limited in any way after created things and human beings have come into existence? In other words, does God necessarily have to maintain his creatures? Is the incarnation of the Logos in the human nature of Jesus a necessary event so that sin can be forgiven? Is God's freedom in any way limited after the formation of the Church?

5. **The relationship of God and creation to the reality of sin.** How is pain, sorrow, sickness, or even violence in nature compatible with a God who is infinitely good? Even more pressing is the question—how has a loving and compassionate God at least allowed human sin and evil to be a part of creation?

Part of the task of this series will be to explore the distinctive approach to these issues within the Franciscan Intellectual Tradition. As will be seen, there is a great difference between the trinitarian theology and the christology developed by Thomas Aquinas and his followers and the trinitarian theology and the christology developed by Bonaventure and John Duns Scotus. There is also a great divergence in these two traditions between the theology of redemption and the theology of sacraments. The divergences include different theologies of creation and sin, including original sin. Even more striking is the different way these traditions relate theology to spirituality. This historical overview, as mentioned above, indicates that in the twelfth and thirteenth centuries Western theologians already possessed a magnificent inheritance. With the new method, philosophical structure and common text, they moved in directions both old and new, both similar and dissimilar. Our focus is now specifically on identifying the central components of the Franciscan Intellectual Tradition. To do this, we must first re-visit the philosophy of Aristotle.

PART THREE
THE PHILOSOPHICAL WORLD
OF ARISTOTLE

A lthough the reader may find the following exposé of Aristotle a little daunting, its importance will become apparent when our Franciscan tradition is examined in more detail. It is also hoped that this brief exposition will help those reading the entire series to understand the primary texts of the Franciscan Intellectual Tradition, which in their academic form use the language and categories outlined in this section. Just as our own cultural world might take as a fundamental framework the insights of scientists, psychologists or sociologists, so the medieval theologian presupposed categories of thought inherited from Aristotle.

The genius of Aristotle was his ability to construct a philosophy that encompassed the entire universe. The foundational philosophical categories, which he developed at great length, include every reality possible. Following Parmenides and Plato, Aristotle selected the term "being" as his fundamental designation of all reality. Everything in the universe, whether in the ontological order (actually) or in the epistemological order (mentally), is "being." The entire world, for Aristotle, is a "being world." Outside the "being world" is absolute non-being. Outside of being there is absolutely nothing.

For Aristotle, this "being world" required an "unmoved mover." Aristotle does not identify the unmoved mover as God, nor does he attribute any *primary efficient causality* (cf. p. 21 below for a definition of efficient causality) to the unmoved mover. Beyond the unmoved mover, all other beings are moveable, but Aristotle does not see the unmoved mover as the "creator" of these moveable beings. The Jewish-Christian understanding of creation has been seen as the prime example of *primary efficient causality*. In Greek philosophy, movability and change denote imperfection. Immovability and unchangeability denote perfection. Plato considered the world of ideas as a world that was immovable and unchanging, and therefore perfect. Aristotle rejects such a world of ideas, but the omnipresence of movable beings in our own world demanded some unmovable being. Aristotle is vague in his description of the "unmoved mover," and scholars are not in agreement as to its correct interpretation in Aristotelian philosophy.

To understand movable beings, however, Aristotle presented a very clear, well defined and all-inclusive manner of "predication." These are called his predicamental categories. In the twelfth and thirteenth centuries, all the theologians used these four predicamental categories to explain various Catholic doctrines. Their doctrinal explanations, in which they used these four categories, included creation itself, the incarnation, the meaning of grace, the theological understanding of the seven sacraments and the role of the Church. An understanding of the Franciscan Intellectual Tradition requires, therefore, a basic understanding of these categories. The Franciscan theological interpretation of some key issues of Catholic doctrine involved the use of these four categories, and it is precisely in the interpretation of these Aristotelian categories that the Franciscan Intellectual Tradition differs significantly from the Dominican Intellectual Tradition.

I.
The Predicamental Categories of Aristotelian Philosophy

Within the "being world," Aristotle establishes his four predicamental categories. These four categories classify the distinct ways in which "being" can be predicated of all reality and of every individual part of reality. "Being" can be predicated of some "thing" or some "being" in one of four ways.

To predicate means:

- **to name something for what it fundamentally is;**
- **to classify something in a basic or fundamental way;**
- **to affirm something in its position within a being world.**

THERE ARE FOUR PREDICAMENTAL CATEGORIES, BUT THEY DIFFER IN IMPORTANCE. THESE FOUR CATEGORIES ARE ALWAYS ARRANGED IN THE FOLLOWING ORDER:

1. SUBSTANCE. Substance is the basic category. To call, name, classify or affirm that this or that "being" is a substance is to call, name, classify and affirm that this or that "being" is essentially a primary entity. Aristotle's definition, cited by many scholastic theologians, reads: *Primary substance is a being that can be defined without reference to anything else.* If you need to use a reference to another reality to explain what this or that being is, you are not talking about a true substance.

An example: In Aristotle, the fundamental essence of a human being is to be a "rational animal," and one does not need to refer to any other specific animal to understand this classification. One does not need to refer to any other rational being to understand this classification. It is by itself the sub-standing being upon which and to which all other references can be made regarding this rational animal, such as existence, personal relations, health, intelligence, age, occupation, etc. All these qualities "reside" in a substance, namely, this particular rational animal.

The next three categories depend on substance. In describing them, the definition of substance as that which can be defined without reference to anything else will become clearer.

2. QUANTITY. Quantity, the second most basic predicamental category, is only understood in terms of reference, namely, two. Quantity makes sense only if you can understand it in terms of **MORE OR LESS**. In some beings there is more quantity, while in other beings there is less quantity. Without a more or less referent, quantity is meaningless. More or less, however, needs specification, e.g., more than "X" but less than "Y." Quantity also needs a reference to a "substance." Quantity expresses a "more" or a "less" **OF** something. Ultimately, that **OF** something needs to be a substance as we explained it in number one above. Some "thing" is more; some "thing" is less.

The **OF** aspect and the **MORE OR LESS** aspect provide meaning to quantity. In other words, it has meaning only in reference to something else **OF** which it is a specification. But quantity has meaning not only in reference to something else of which it is a specification; it has meaning since it states the **MORE OR LESS** of this specification. The "something else" is the substrate for these relationships, of which quantity is descriptive in a more or less way. Quantity adheres in something, and quantity is compared to something else in a more or less way.

The **ACTUAL QUANTITY** of something is purely accidental, since it could be more or it could be less, or it might not even be at all. Quantity does not have the "foundational" aspect that substance has. However, quantity is foundational (along with substance) for the next two predicamental categories.

3. QUALITY. Quality is not about more or less; rather, it is about an attribute, a characteristic and a trait that something has. Quality can only have meaning when it refers to something else. Quality is an attribute or characteristic **OF** some "thing." It is a quality of some thing, however, only in an accidental way. The thing of which it is a quality, that is, the substance of which it is a quality, can continue to exist without this quality. However, the quality cannot exist nor have any meaning whatsoever unless it is related to a substantial being.

Moreover, qualities, characteristics and traits can be **MORE OR LESS.** A human person can be more or less mature. Maturity is a quality, but one can be more mature or less mature. Qualities have primary foundation in substance, and secondary foundation in quantity.

4. RELATION. Relation is the last and the least of the predicamental categories in Aristotle's philosophical system. The reason it is last and least is this: it has no being simply by itself. A relation only has meaning when there is a situation in which "X" is relating to "Y" and "Y" is relating to "X." Were one to remove either "X" or "Y" from the equation, then "X" is not relating to "Y" and "Y" is not relating to "X" with the result that there is no longer any relationship at all. To say: "I am relating," but there is no one nor any thing to which you are relating is meaningless. There simply is no relating, even though you are saying "I am relating." In Latin, the being of a relationship is called *esse ad*. It is a being (*esse*) only when it is "of and to (*ad*)" something. Remove the "of" and "to" and relation has no *esse*, no being, at all. In this way, relation for Aristotle is the least and the last of the four categorical predicaments.

These are the foundational categories, the predicamental categories, by which Aristotle analyzes the entire universe of being. "Category" is the English translation of a Greek word that actually means "predicate." How do we *predicate* aspects of being *to each other*? This is Aristotle's first question. The second question is what do we *mean by predicates*? The first question *distinguishes beings from each other by way of their relationship*. The second question *focuses on the "what" (the quiddity), of each predicate taken by itself.*

The internal connection of the four categories is thus two-fold. Even though substance is to be defined without a relationship to anything else, it is the first of the categories, implying a second, third, etc. Quality, quantity and relationship are also established as second, third and last. All four categories, however, express something about "what" each category is by itself. As we shall see, the Franciscan Intellectual Tradition, in using all of the categories of Aristotle, emphasizes in a special way that of relationality.

THE GENIUS OF ARISTOTLE lies in his philosophical system of the four categories. Every being, whether the being is real or only imaginary, is either substance, quantity, quality, or relationship. Nothing exists that is not one of these four classifications. Substance is a being that can be defined without a relationship to anything else. Quantity, quality and relation are understood only in relationship to something else. This four-fold classification of all beings properly refers to actual, existing beings. By extension, the four-fold classification of being also refers to the mental beings that are only in our mind and in our imagination.

II.
The Four Types of Causality in
Aristotle's Philosophy

The basic interaction of all beings in the philosophy of Aristotle (substance, quality, quantity and relation) is through causality. Beings relate, in a causal way, to one another through different types of causality. The writings of Aristotle describe four basic types of causality, and through this the "Being world" of Aristotle is then portrayed as a unified "Being world." The four types of cause can be expressed by the following diagram:

1. EFFICIENT CAUSE. An efficient cause is a cause that brings into existence the very being of the effect. This does not mean that an efficient cause only creates something out of nothing. Rather, something does not exist unless it has an efficient cause. Mothers and fathers efficiently cause the conception of their children. Fire efficiently causes destruction.

2. MATERIAL CAUSE. A material cause is that which allows prime matter to bring something material into being. Prime matter represents the ultimate foundation for all material things, whether existent or imagined. In its primary state of being it has no specific form but it is the principle that accounts for the material element in our universe.

3. FORMAL CAUSE. A formal cause is that which allows both non-material and material beings to have some sort of intelligent form. Without this intelligent form, one cannot know them. A formless being is a non-being. Plato had provided for "eternal forms" to exist in "heaven." These eternal forms provide the model and the matrix for all non-eternal forms. Aristotle rejects such eternal forms. Actual forms exist only in actual beings. Human intelligence can "abstract" the form from its actual state of being and unite it to other such abstracted forms in the human mind and thus know that something is a "human being," a "tree," or an "animal."

4. FINAL CAUSE. The final cause is operative because a given being is moving towards its purpose. This causality is a "luring" or "enticing" part of a being's development. Final cause has a certain future-related aspect, but Aristotle wishes to state that the final cause is operative in the present as the dynamism luring or enticing a being to move towards its goal.

THE GENIUS OF ARISTOTLE continues in his careful classification of all causality. These four types of causality have profoundly influenced Western thought from the twelfth century to the present twenty-first century. Modern science has called into question this manner of describing causality, but Aristotle's views are still prevalent in the Western world.

The Franciscan Intellectual Tradition, as well as the Dominican Intellectual Tradition, used these four ways of causality to explain the theological meaning of creation, i.e., God is the efficient cause *par excellence*, since God alone can create (efficiently cause) something to come from nothing. In the theology of the sacraments, especially in the explanation of the real presence of Jesus in the bread and wine, one finds in both traditions some form of causality. In both traditions, God is the main efficient cause that makes Jesus really present at the Eucharist, but there is a cooperative action by the minister of the sacrament. For the Dominicans, the cooperative action is united to the efficient causality of God, namely, an instrumental efficient causality by the minister. The minister, in a very secondary way, co-acts efficiently although instrumentally, with the overriding efficient causality of God.

For the Franciscans, who wanted nothing to do with a mixture of the divine and human in efficient causality, two approaches were developed. Bonaventure developed a form of "moral causality." This means that the minister prays that God will efficiently act. The minister's prayer is described as a "moral influence," voiced by the minister on behalf of the community, petitioning God to act in an efficient way. Scotus went even further, stating that all the actions of the sacramental ministers and communities are only an "occasional" cause. This means that the Christian community is celebrating Eucharist (and all other sacraments) in a basic format that God has enjoined. When the Christian community acts together at a given occasion in obedience to God, God gives grace and makes Jesus present. God acts, not because we, the community and the ministers, do anything causative. By our following of God's will, we are simply presenting an "occasion" which God has asked us to do. For Scotus, the free determination of God is absolute. We do nothing except follow the ways that the absolutely free God has determined.

On this issue of causality, the theological understanding in the Franciscan Intellectual Tradition and the Dominican Intellectual Tradition are miles apart, with the Franciscan Intellectual Tradition emphasizing a very modified form of human participation in the grace-filled action of God.

III.
The Comprehensive Structure of
Aristotelian Philosophy

The following diagram represents the philosophical world of Aristotle, a world based on "being" with categories that compartmentalize every possible form of being. The diagram does not express the intricacies of Aristotle's philosophy; it is, rather, a generalized statement. Aristotle, in his own work *Treatise on Categories*, indicates that the categories themselves are not complex expressions. All the major medieval theologians accepted these categories of being, modified them in two major areas, and then used them in their theological presentations in various degrees of intensity. Since the categories are an all-inclusive description of being, the categories are both epistemological and ontological. They are an expression of how one thinks of being and beings (*epistemological*); they are an expression of the "quiddity" of what being and beings are in reality (*ontological*).

BEING

UNMOVED MOVER = UNMOVED BEING =
UNCHANGEABLE BEING

MOVABLE BEINGS
THE CHANGEABLE BEINGS IN OUR UNIVERSE

ESSENCE
The categorical definition of what an individual being
in our universe is in an unchangeable, though limited, way

NATURE
The same essence considered as a principle of an action

SUBSTANCE
The first and most basic of all categories
Primary substance is that essence or that nature that can
be defined without reference to any other being.

QUANTITY
The aspect of moveable
being that is measurable in
terms of greater, less, or
equal or in terms of
increase/decrease in
magnitude

QUALITY
The aspect of being that in
an accidental way affects a
substance or nature and
can only be or exist in a
substance. It cannot exist
or be on its own

RELATION
For Aristotle this is *the least of all beings.*
It exists only when there is a connection
that unites two other beings.

IV.
Two Major Changes Made by
Thirteenth-century Catholic Theologians
in Their Acceptance of Aristotelian Philosophy

THE FIRST MAJOR CHANGE
OF ARISTOTLE'S PHILOSOPHY
made by the medieval scholastic theologians

GOD
IS CALLED
BEING ITSELF, ESSE IPSUM, INFINITE BEING
and
THE CREATOR OF ALL OTHER BEINGS,
THE EFFICIENT CAUSE, THE FINAL CAUSE OF ALL
OTHER BEINGS.

Theologians based this position on Catholic Faith,
on the Old and New Testaments and on the constant teaching
of the Church, which portrays God
as the Creator of all things.

Aristotle did not call the unmoved mover God
nor did Aristotle see the unmoved mover either as an
efficient cause or as a creator.
Finite beings, for Aristotle, had always been in existence
and would remain in existence forever.

THE SECOND MAJOR CHANGE
OF ARISTOTLE'S PHILOSOPHY
made by the medieval scholastic theologians

**ALL OTHER BEINGS ARE
CREATED BY GOD.**

To call all other beings finite, limited, and contingent
is primarily a philosophical position.

To call the same beings "created" is a theological position,
since it is a matter of faith to believe in a Creator God.

The scholastic introduction of "God" into Aristotle's
philosophical framework means that
philosophy and theology
are related in scholastic theology.

The scholastic theologians based their position
in the same way as the change noted above,
namely, on Catholic Faith,
on the Old and New Testaments,
and on the constant teaching of the Church.

The philosophy of Aristotle does not include a
theology either of God or of God as Creator of all things.

All of the major theologians from the eleventh century to the fourteenth century rejected the position of Aristotle that did not truly include a place for a personal "God" and for a "Creator God." In this rejection of major aspects in the philosophy of Aristotle, we see that the medieval scholars accepted his philosophy but only in a very judicious way, changing it when the philosophical positions contradicted a basic Christian doctrine. Catholic Faith came first; the philosophy of Aristotle, second.

Aristotle's concept of being was changed to include God as being itself. In turn, this adaptation required an altered philosophical interpretation of Aristotle's understanding of changeable beings. That these beings were changeable was not the issue. That these beings were created was the issue. In Aristotle's system, there was no beginning or ending of changeable beings. Moveable beings in some form or another were "eternal." If beings were durationally infinite, which scholastic theologians found to be contradictory to Scripture and Church doctrine, Aristotle's unmoved mover could not be a creator. Creation is a creation from nothing, *creatio ex nihilo*; but if a state of nothingness never existed and if changeable beings in some form or another always existed, the theological belief in creation is fundamentally excluded.

The following diagram highlights the two basic areas in Aristotle's philosophy that these theologians changed. The diagram essentially reprints the previous diagram (cf. p. 24) but the shaded areas mark the precise areas of the theologians' basic changes. These same theologians, in the thirteenth and fourteenth centuries, by and large accepted the remainder of Aristotle's philosophy and used his predicamental categories to interpret Catholic Faith. Even today we have many indications of this use of Aristotle in Catholic theology. The manner in which individual medieval theologians used the categories of Aristotle and extent to which they used them differ, but they all employed Aristotle's ideas in one way or another.

GOD = INFINITE BEING and *ESSE IPSUM*
GOD IS UNCREATED AND ETERNAL
AND THE CREATOR OF ALL OTHER BEINGS

THEREFORE

ALL FINITE BEINGS ARE CREATED,
CONTINGENT AND TEMPORAL

ALL MOVABLE BEINGS ARE CREATED BY GOD
AND CLASSIFIED BY ONE OF THESE CATEGORIES

ESSENCE
The categorical definition of what an individual being
is in an unchangeable way

NATURE
The essence considered as a principle of an action

SUBSTANCE
The first and most basic of all categories
Primary substance is that which can be defined
without reference to any other being.

ALL FINITE SUBSTANCES ARE CREATED,
CONTINGENT AND TEMPORAL

QUANTITY
The aspect of being that is
measurable in terms of
greater or less, equal or of
increasing or decreasing
magnitude

QUALITY
The aspect of being that
accidentally affects a
substantial essence but not
in a quiddative way.

ALL FINITE QUANTITIES AND ALL FINITE QUALITIES
ARE CREATED, CONTINGENT AND TEMPORAL

RELATION
The least of all beings,
a connection which unites two other beings

ALL FINITE RELATIONS ARE CREATED,
CONTINGENT AND TEMPORAL.

A few comments on each of these two changes need to be made, since both of them are central to Christian theology itself, and not simply to a theological tradition.

A. GOD AS SUPREME BEING, *ESSE IPSUM*

Scholastic theologians described God in terms of being, but since the manner of being in God is totally different from the manner in which all finite things and people are beings, God is fundamentally described as being itself, *esse ipsum*. No creature is or can be *being itself*. All creatures are created, contingent and temporal. God alone is infinite being; all creatures are finite beings. Thus, the predicamental categories of substance, quantity, quality and relation do not apply to being itself, to infinite being, to God. All other beings, however, must be classified as substances or quantities or qualities or relations; and, for the scholastics, all of these categories are created, contingent and temporal. Aristotle would not have used these designations for unchangeable being.

B. THE ETERNITY OF THE FINITE UNIVERSE

The issue of the eternity of a universe of changeable beings did present some hesitations. Both Thomas Aquinas and John Duns Scotus realized that one could argue *logically* that finite, created and contingent beings of themselves did not have to have either a beginning or an ending. Other major theologians of the twelfth and thirteenth centuries did not accept this position of "durational infinity." Thomas and Scotus saw a logical possibility for durational infinity of changeable beings, but since revelation and Church doctrine included the creation of our universe by God, they, together with all other major theologians of that time, rejected this aspect of Aristotle's position on the actual eternity of the universe. In other words, Aristotle argued that the sum of all realities, not individual realities, was durationally without beginning or end. This kind of reality was durationally infinite.

Since God in the Jewish-Christian sacred writings is clearly presented as a creator, all of the medieval theologians taught that there was an actual beginning of all finite creatures. Basing themselves on the same Scriptures, they also taught that there would be an ending of at least some creatures. However, to angels and human beings

God has given the grace of immortality, *a totally unmerited gift*. Neither angels nor humans have any aspect of their being which is intrinsically incapable of death or destruction. Angels and human beings are finite, contingent and temporal by their very nature. Angels and human beings cannot claim immortal life, everlasting life, or eternal life on the basis that their "eternal soul" or that their essences by their very nature could not be annihilated. Eternal life is a gift from God, not an inalienable right of angelic or human nature.

Given these two explanations on the changes the Christian theologians made in the philosophy of Aristotle, medieval professors at the faculty of arts in the universities, particularly after the middle of the thirteenth century, were very keen on teaching the philosophy of Aristotle. Their courses were central to the philosophical curriculum. A student had to enroll in the arts program and graduate in a successful way. Only then was a student eligible (providing he was a cleric) to begin theological studies. Consequently, all the great theologians of the thirteenth century were well-grounded in Aristotelian philosophy before they began their studies in theology. They all entered the theological curriculum with a competent knowledge of Aristotle's philosophy. But, as in all fields of study, even today, some students had learned well, while others did not have the same penetrating insights. This depth or this mediocrity can be found in the various theological writings of scholastic theologians, whether they were Franciscan, Dominican, Augustinian, or diocesan.

The Franciscan Intellectual Tradition includes theologians who had studied Aristotelian philosophy in a penetrating way. Moreover, some of these Franciscan theologians used their philosophy generously in their theological writings; others were more reluctant to do this. Among Franciscan scholars, then, one finds both a generous acceptance and a cautious acceptance of Aristotle's philosophy and both a widespread and a selective use of it. The use and acceptance of Aristotle is not monolithic. For example, Bonaventure, who knew Aristotle well, is selective in his use of Aristotle's thought. Scotus, for his part, uses Aristotle abundantly and creatively. Yet, the works of both Bonaventure and Scotus were key to the formation of the Franciscan Intellectual Tradition. Given this background, it is now possible for us to turn to the formation of the Franciscan Intellectual Tradition, its foundation in Francis of Assisi and its articulation through the Franciscan masters in their encounter with Aristotle.

PART FOUR
THE GRADUAL DEVELOPMENT
OF THE FRANCISCAN
INTELLECTUAL TRADITION

There were only twelve Franciscan brothers in 1208/1209. By 1250 there were thirty thousand Franciscan friars.[1] This was a remarkable growth for any religious order in the Catholic Church. Both the spiritual and intellectual training of the applicants, novices and young friars became an immediate necessity, given the large numbers of men entering the ranks of the Franciscan community. From almost the very beginning, Franciscan formation, Franciscan mission and Franciscan study were linked in the emerging Order's identity. How were young friars to be trained? How were they to be intellectually formed? How could the tools of the intellectual world of the universities be brought to converge with the profound spiritual insights and vision of Francis and Clare of Assisi? How could study support evangelization? Hidden in these issues confronting the community, we can discern the outlines of the development of the Franciscan Intellectual Tradition and its profound desire to be faithful to the intuitions of the Saints of Assisi.

It is not surprising that the intellectual formation of Franciscans became an issue of immediate concern. Internally, in the decades immediately after 1208/1209, the Franciscans did not have within their ranks a large number of men qualified to educate and form the growing number of applicants, novices and recently vowed Franciscans. Within a very short time, the early friars began to live in two of the major university cities of the era—Oxford and Paris. At first, they did not establish schools, but simply friaries in which those in formation could live. The cities were places where the friars could evangelize. Eventually, especially after the entrance of some learned clerics, those in formation began to attend classes at the university itself. These students, at the beginning of their academic work, studied under the masters in the faculty of arts (philosophy). Only after successfully matriculating through the arts program did they move on to instruction by the faculty of theology. At that time, the study of theology was reserved to clerics. Lay men and women could not enroll in the theological programs of the universities. All the early Franciscan theologians, then, were clerics— seminarians at first and then ordained priests.

Student friars at the University of Paris arrived as early as 1219. They lived at first with the Benedictines at St. Denis, but soon after acquired their own Franciscan residence. Student friars arrived at the University of Oxford around 1224 and established a Franciscan residence.

From this perspective, we will look at the gradual development of the Franciscan Intellectual Tradition by moving in the following way:

I.   We will reflect on the very foundation for the Franciscan Intellectual Tradition, namely, the spirituality and vision of St. Francis and St. Clare.
II. We will consider the lineage of the first Franciscan theologians at the University of Paris and at the University of Oxford.
III. We will identify other important and highly educated Franciscans whose careers did not culminate in teaching positions at either Oxford or Paris.

I.   The Franciscan Foundation: The Spirituality and Vision of St. Francis (1181/82-1226) and St. Clare (1193-1253)

The spirituality and vision of Francis and Clare found its theological expression in the teachings of Franciscan scholars at the Universities at Paris and Oxford. Without this spirituality and vision there would be no Franciscan Intellectual Tradition. One of the major Franciscan scholars in the first half of the twentieth century was Éphrem Longpré, a Friar Minor from the French-speaking province in Québec. It was his view that one of most important core elements of the spiritual vision of St. Francis was his astounding insight into the depth and height, the width and length of the incarnation. In this introductory volume, we build our synthesis around this insight. Longpré writes:

The spirituality of St. Francis of Assisi can neither be described nor delineated on the one hand, or, on the other hand, it can neither be interpreted nor thought through independent of the religious experience which was a revelation to Francis, after he had left his more worldly ways, the mystery of Jesus Christ, especially the crucified Lord, (Bonaventure, *Legenda maior*, 1:5, 13:10) for this revelation had made of him a "new evangelist" (I Celano, 89) and the "herald of Christian perfection" (*Legenda maior*, prologue, 1). In Francis' spirituality everything follows in a very unified way and with a certain logic from this encounter with Christ. This encounter with Christ was not a sudden situation, but a gradual one, beginning with his entry into the army and the "vision of Christ" in Spoleto, and peaking (initially) with his encounter with Christ in the chapel of San Damiano (autumn 1205).[2]

This spiritual vision of Francis encompasses two realities: *the humility of the incarnation* and *the love of the passion*. In *The Life of St. Francis* by Thomas of Celano, written in 1229, we read:

> Francis used to recall with regular meditation the word of Christ and recollect His deeds with most attentive perception. Indeed, so thoroughly did the humility of the incarnation and the love of the passion occupy his memory that he scarcely wanted to think of anything else.[3]

In the introduction to Celano's *The Life of St. Francis*, the editors note "that the theme of 'the humility of the incarnation' uniquely identifies Book One as Thomas summarizes *the conversion, life, teaching and example of Francis*."[4] Celano, in this first book, finds that the humility of the incarnation is the key issue, which relates all aspects of Francis's life. It is a key issue in the spiritual vision of the Poverello. In the next paragraph, the same editors inform us: "In Book Two the love of the passion predominates."[5] The transforming experience of Francis on Mt. Alverno is one of burning and intimate love, a love for God in the presence of a crucified Jesus.

An understanding of these two themes, the humility of the incarnation and the love of the passion, will help us grasp the deepest dimensions of Francis's spiritual vision, a vision he shared with St. Clare.

A. *The Humility of the Incarnation*

Thousands of theological books have been written about Jesus. When we read them, we learn about the divinity of Jesus, the sovereignty of Jesus and the power and majesty of Jesus. Most of these theological books deliberately stress issues of greatness. The theme of the humility of the incarnation is briefly mentioned but does not play a central role. The primary lens through which Jesus is presented in these volumes is not the humility of the incarnation. Rather, these volumes exalt Jesus. For instance, a contemporary resurrection christology stresses the role of the Resurrection, Ascension (exaltation) and sending of the Holy Spirit. From the standpoint of the Resurrection-Ascension, we are able to understand the very meaning of his life, message and death, and we also see the value of the Church as it has lived out and is living out the Jesus-event.

For Francis, it is not the Resurrection of Jesus that offers such a lens. In many ways, it is not the divinity of Jesus alone which centers his vision. It is certainly not the Jesus who alone offered satisfaction for all our sins (the atonement theory regarding Christ's death) that centers his focus. Nor can one say that it is simply the incarnation which centers his view. It is the incarnation, but, more precisely, it is the *humility of the incarnation* which summarizes the *life, conversion, teaching and example* of Francis.

An incident from the life of Francis helps us to understand the depth of his meditations on the humility of the incarnation.[6] In 1194, the Empress Constance was on her way to Sicily to join her husband Henry VI, the Holy Roman Emperor. She was pregnant at that time, and she realized that her labor pains had begun in earnest. The entourage decided that she should go to the nearby town of Jesi and there give birth to her child. The infant, a boy, was baptized in the Cathedral of San Rufino in Assisi, and he later became the Holy Roman Emperor, Frederick II.

At the time of Empress Constance's stay in Assisi, Francis was about thirteen years old, a teenager. One can easily imagine the excitement that the presence of the empress caused, not only for the teenagers of Jesi and Assisi, but for all the citizens of these towns. Knights on horseback and in sun-reflecting armor rode into the city. Coaches, bearing the important people of Lady Constance's entourage, followed one after the other. Finally, the coach bearing the empress arrived with a large escort of knights on horses. Francis, like everyone else at that time, heard detail after detail of this visit, including the birth of this boy in nearby Jesi and the baptism of the child in his own hometown. The whole of Assisi was eager to hear all the particulars. Clearly, Francis had been all ears and eyes as well.

We hear another part of this story in the well-known celebration of Christmas at Greccio. Fifteen days before Christmas, Francis instructed a man named John in the following way:

> If you desire to celebrate the coming feast of the Lord together at Greccio—he said to him—hurry before me and carefully make ready the things I tell you. For I wish to enact the memory of that babe who was born in Bethlehem; to see as much as is possible with my own bodily eyes the discomfort of his infant needs, how he lay in a manger, and how, with an ox and an ass standing by, he rested on hay (1Celano 30:84).

When Christmas day came, Francis arrived, and what he saw made him very glad.

> Simplicity is given a place of honor, poverty is exalted, humility is commended, and out of Greccio is made a new Bethlehem. . . . [Francis] preaches to the people standing around him and pours forth sweet honey about the birth of the poor King and the poor city of Bethlehem (1Celano 30: 85-6)

Perhaps—and only perhaps—Francis thought of the Holy Roman Emperor's birth and baptism. God, the emperor of the universe, became a human child on this earth of ours; but when Jesus-God was born, there were no knights on horseback, no trumpets and drums, no coaches with elegant horses and costumed drivers. In fact, Francis realized that God entered the town called Bethlehem in a quiet, humble, almost unknown way. What a contrast to Lady Constance and her newborn child, Frederick.

These two instances are important for an understanding of Francis's understanding of the humility of the incarnation. A mere human empress and a mere future emperor had come to Assisi with all that gold might buy at the time. People fawned over the mother and the child. But when God became flesh in the womb of Mary and was born in Bethlehem, no pomp and circumstance attended this unbelievable event. The gospels relate that shepherds, who were equivalent to the gypsies of later centuries, were the first to visit this mother and child. Most of the Jewish people at the time of Jesus despised and looked down on shepherds. Shepherds represented no important Jewish person or group. In fact, no important Jewish person or group came to Bethlehem to see God-made-flesh. The same gospels describe the visit by the magi. These men were not Jewish; they were *goyim*, i.e., pagans or infidels. In other words, the Jewish world of Palestine continued with absolutely no official recognition of this pregnancy and birth.

Francis realized that God loved our world and wanted to be with us. God did not become incarnate as some mighty lord. It is the humility of the incarnation that is central to Francis's vision. Creation, for him, was a powerful, living mural of God's love. The sun was not simply a large star; the sun was Francis's own brother, Brother Sun. The moon was not simply a large asteroid; the moon for Francis was his own sister, Sister Moon. In fact, each part of the created universe in the vision of Francis was a loving gift of God and a creature whose very existence praised God. One could easily say that God's presence in and through creation itself is a mini-incarnation and that God's presence in the humanness of Jesus is a maxi-incarnation. Both the presence of God in the created universe itself and the presence of God in Jesus are incarnationally interrelated.

They are also creationally interrelated. This relationship became one of the essential elements in Franciscan theology and philosophy, in Franciscan spirituality and in Franciscan pastoral life in the Church. For Francis, even the Eucharist has an incarnational relationship. At each Eucharist, God becomes really present. At a given Eucharist, God is present in a unique part of our created world with unique, individualized human beings at a uniquely sacramental moment. The God who is present at such a unique Eucharist is the same God who created all things and who is present, incarnationally, in the human nature of Jesus. One might picture the simple church of the Portiuncula at the time of Francis and imagine the Eucharist being celebrated there with poor people gathered around the altar. In such a picture, one catches another glimpse of the humility of the incarnation.

Francis's love for Mary is also due to Mary's example of the humility of the incarnation. She was the Mother of God, but she never boasted about her election. Mary is an integral part of the humility of the incarnation. The Church, with all its limitations, is truly Church when it reflects the *humility of the incarnation*. Francis loved the Church because he saw beyond the scandals and corruption of the medieval Church. He found a Church deeply reflecting the humility of the incarnation. Francis honored lepers, since they, too, share in the humility of the incarnation. Beggars, marginalized people and even those shunned by the civil or ecclesiastical powers were, for Francis, examples of the humility of the incarnation. They were his "Brother and Sister Beggars," his "Brother and Sister Marginalized" and his "Brother and Sister politically or ecclesiastically shunned." Francis saw the presence and love of God in all of these. They might have been robbers, but he still called them "Brother Robbers."

The breadth of the humility of the incarnation is brought out by another moment in Francis's life. In 1219, Francis, with perhaps twelve other brothers, sailed to Candia in Cyprus and then to Acre (St. Jean d'Acre) in Palestine.[7] Sometime after the defeat of the crusaders, Francis decided to go to see the Sultan, Malik-al-Kamil. He did this without the blessing of Cardinal Pelagius, the legate of the pope during this crusade. Francis, with another friar, Brother Illuminato, went on foot from Damietta to the city of Mansura in Egypt. Both friars were apprehended by Muslim soldiers and physically abused. Francis, however, kept calling out the name of Malik-al-Kamil, so the soldiers decided to take them to the sultan's headquarters, thinking they might be legates of the crusader leadership. The two men met—Malik-al-Kamil, a devout follower of Islam, and Francis, a devout follower of Jesus. In the course of their discussions, each came to respect the other, a respect based on the religious depth which each saw in the other. The texts describing this encounter do not say that Francis called the Sultan, my brother, Malik-al-Kamil. The texts, however, do indicate that the two men truly respected each other. Both perceived the presence of God's holiness in each other. For Francis this was an insight into the humility of the incarnation. The Word of God entered our earth. In the humanity of Jesus, the Word lived out our own human way of life, sharing our earth-world, breathing our air and mingling with all sorts of people. Jesus himself experienced the presence of God in those who were marginalized and even humiliated.

In all of this there are ramifications attached to a focus on the humility of the incarnation. The entire earth, just as it is, is a gospel of divine presence. What is more awesome is the humble presence of God, in people and in things, that goes unnoticed. The humility of the incarnation is itself an incarnation of humility. The love and presence of the incarnate Word of God affects the whole earth, and the widespread love and presence express the depth and height, the breadth and length of the humility of the incarnation. In the infidel, in the pagan and non-Christian Malik-Al-Kamil, Francis of Assisi experienced the humble presence of God, the mystery of the humble incarnation.

The meeting of Francis and Malik-Al-Kamil has had a strong affect on the inter-religious dialogues that are taking place today. The way in which Francis of Assisi related to a man of a different religion offers an alternative way of facing someone who is not a Christian. The key word in this manner of encounter is, of course, *respect*, or more clearly stated: *a respect for the presence of holiness in the other*. In many ways, such a respect is based on the humility of the incarnation. Just as shepherds and magi were present at the crib and home of Jesus, and thus shared in the humility of the incarnation itself, so, too, in Muslims, in Hindus, in Buddhists, in Daoists, etc., one experiences the presence of the holy God, incarnated again in a most humble a way.

As we have seen, the humility of the incarnation stretches out to all of creation. Francis had a marvelous respect for animals of all kinds, for the sun, the moon, and the stars, for water, wind, fire, and for the earth itself. The environment in which he lived was an environment that praised God. For Francis, it was not only a question of our praising God through Brother Sun and Sister Moon, for Brother Sun and Sister Moon already are giving praise to God just by being sun and moon. Francis merely came to understand, hear and see the sun and the moon praising God.

In today's world, the environmental issues are serious and severe. The earth itself has been abused and raped. Little respect has been given to habitat and limited resources, to dying species and to the human relationships between nature and human life. In the name of money, natural beauty and natural resources are being absorbed into the machinery of greed. God's creation, however, is incarnationally related to the presence of God in our entire world, and yet we find these created gifts of God being squandered and selfishly abused. In the Franciscan vision, the created world may actually be squandered and abused, but because of God the Creator's presence in these created gifts, Francis and Franciscans can still address Brother Squandered Forest, Sister Squandered Ocean, etc. Even in their squandered state, they are still our brothers and sisters, not because of us, but because, like us, they have been created and gifted by one and the same Holy-Father-God. The sinner is still my brother the sinner or my sister the sinner, and both deserve my respect. So, too, an environment that shows the ravages of abuse is still a gift of God and merits respect. Even in an abused creation, God is present in an incarnationally related way. When people become aware of God's presence in the environment, they need to think twice about how they use it. When they see that the misuse and abuse of the environment leaves thousands of poor people mired more deeply in poverty, they need to think not twice but many times.

B. The Love of the Passion

A second part of this spiritual vision of Francis of Assisi is *the love of the passion*. The insight here is the central and essential connection of love, on the one hand, and the suffering and death of Jesus, on the other. Two German Franciscan scholars, Cajetan Esser and Engelbert Grau, expressed this love for the passion as follows:

> It was especially in the passion and sufferings of Christ that Francis marveled most at the humility of God, for therein God lowered himself to the very dregs! . . . Not only did he sympathize in a human way with his suffering Lord by tears and lament, but he was likewise filled with grateful joy and jubilation at the redemption which the most holy Father had wrought in the world through the Passion of his Son.[8]

In one's daily life, there are many instances in which husbands and wives have risked their lives for one another and in which mothers and fathers have risked their lives for their children. On many occasions, a spouse or parent has died in order that the other spouse or the child might live. Such a death is an expression of how much spouses love each other, of how much parents love their children. Even the slow death of growing old is an expression of love, since parents grow old as they work hard to provide for their children. We can apply this same sort of reflection to our understanding of the love of the passion. Many Christians might meditate on the crucified Lord and even shed tears, but the reason that is often given is that Jesus suffered so much because we have sinned. Sin is the focus point of the arrest, conviction and death of Jesus. This view of the "sacrifice" of the cross dominates the Western theology of the cross. For Francis, it is God's love that dominates. In the humility of the incarnation, Jesus loved us so much that he even suffered and died to show us how much God loves us. As the Gospel of John expresses it: He loved us unto the end, that is, the end of his life (Jn. 13:1).

In the first twelve chapters of John's gospel, the word "life" appears again and again. From chapter thirteen to chapter twenty, the word "love" dominates. Raymond Brown, a major New Testament scholar, in his commentary on John's gospel, reminds us that if we wish to understanding the meaning of the death of Jesus in John's gospel, we must go first to the washing of the disciple's feet. This washing of the feet is the symbol, for John, of the entire arrest, trial and death of Jesus.[9] The washing of the feet is clearly a symbol of love, and love is the key to the passion and death of Jesus. It is precisely this aspect of Jesus' death that has focused the vision of St. Francis on the love of the passion.

In the Franciscan Intellectual Tradition, these two ideas, the humility of the incarnation and the love of the passion, have been central. The incarnation, as we shall see, is so central that it is related to first creation, to ongoing creation and to the future, which we call risen life. The love of the passion is also central. The passion or suffering extends not only to the crucifixion of Jesus but also to the suffering of the crucified people at the margins of society. In theology, the terms "incarnation and redemption" are the usual centering points for all christologies. The Franciscan vision of "creation-incarnation-redemption-glory" as intrinsically inter-united is a vision that comes from the gospels themselves, from the early Church Fathers and from early medieval theologians. It initially received a systematic in-depth treatment in the thirteenth century through the writings of the first Franciscan masters, Alexander of Hales, Bonaventure and John Duns Scotus. Let us move then to the formulation of this theological vision of Francis of Assisi in terms more associated with our "academic theological tradition."

II. The First Franciscan Theologians at the Universities of Paris and Oxford

Since the end of the thirteenth century, as indicated above, there has been a form of theology called "Franciscan." The roots of this tradition are present in the New Testament, in the Church Fathers and in early, pre-thirteenth-century medieval theologians. Franciscan theology did not start with the Franciscans. That this theology is now called "Franciscan" indicates that the early Franciscan schoolmen did a masterful job in synthesizing many of the elements that they inherited from previous generations. They drew upon one of the major traditions in Christian history found in the New Testament and the Fathers of the Church and enriched it in such a way that history itself has given this enriched tradition a new name— *Franciscan Theology.*

The following pages indicate the key Franciscans and their mentors at the University of Paris and at the University of Oxford. It is obvious that the intellectual expression of the Franciscan Theological Tradition became a major expression of Christian faith in a very short time after the first friars arrived at these centers of learning. The very number and importance of these friar theologians indicate that the Franciscan Intellectual Tradition began on a solid and respected foundation.

THE FRANCISCAN SCHOOL
AT THE UNIVERSITY OF PARIS

ALEXANDER of HALES

Alexander was born in Hales Owen in Gloucestershire around 1185. He studied in the faculty of arts and of theology at the University of Paris. In 1220 he became a regent master. When the young Franciscans arrived for studies at Paris, it was Alexander who became their main teacher. Through him, these young friars learned that their spirituality could be united to their theological studies. In 1236/7, Alexander became a Franciscan. At that time, he felt no need to change his theology. The spirituality of the Franciscan students had attracted him in a profound way, and it was he who in his classes began to harmonize the Franciscan vision and academic theology. Even as a diocesan priest-professor, he aided the first group of Franciscan masters in the composition of a *Summa theologiae*. Even though he was not the only author of this commentary on the *Sentences*, the work has gained the name of *Summa Alexandri*. He was highly responsible for the introduction of Aristotle and the use of the *Sentences* at the University of Paris. The scholars at Quarrachi noted that without his work in these two areas, scholars such as Thomas Aquinas, Bonaventure and John Duns Scotus might never have appeared. All three of them were dependent on Aristotle and Peter Lombard. The Franciscan Intellectual Tradition owes much to the efforts of this scholarly gentleman. He died in 1245, and his funeral was celebrated by the papal legate, Odo of Chateauroux.

JOHN of LA ROCHELLE

John, who came from La Rochelle, was an avid student of Alexander of Hales. He was born sometime around 1200. He pursued his master of theology at the University of Paris, and Alexander was one of his main professors. When he completed his theological studies at the University of Paris, he became an assistant to Alexander and, in 1238, succeeded him as regent master. He was the first Franciscan to be a regent master at the Franciscan house of studies in Paris. His principal writing is the *Summa de anima* (a *Summa on the Soul*). He followed and developed the thought of Avicenna as regards human knowing. He developed the position of Alexander that there are three

cognitive faculties: reason, which analyzes spiritual beings; understanding, which focuses on created beings; and intelligence, which
studies uncreated being. He emphasized the need for studies and
for culture and had no use for anti-intellectualism. He is one of the
main authors of the *Summa Alexandri*. His death occurred in 1245.

ODO RIGALDUS

Odo Rigaldus (Eudes Rigaud) was born sometime around 1205 and
died in 1275. As a Franciscan student at the University of Paris, he
studied under Alexander of Hales. From 1243 to 1245, he lectured at
the University of Paris on the *Sentences* of Peter Lombard. From Sep-
tember 1245 to early 1248, he was regent master at the Franciscan
school at Paris, succeeding friar John of La Rochelle. There are some
additions to the *Summa Alexandri* that are attributed to Odo Rigaldus.
His *Commentary on the Sentences* is a bridge between Peter Lombard's
positions, which he drew upon, and the teachings of Bonaventure,
who was his student. In 1248, he became the archbishop of Rouen
and was active politically under Louis IX and ecclesiastically at the
Council of Lyon in 1274.

WILLIAM of MELITONA

William of Melitona (Middleton) was one of the early friars to receive a master in theology at Paris. He was a student of Alexander
of Hales. From 1248 to 1253, he was regent master at the Franciscan
house in Paris, succeeding Odo Rigaldus. Most of his academic life
centered on the University of Paris. William is often mentioned as
one of the compilers of the *Summa Alexandri*. He died in 1260.

BONAVENTURE of BAGNOREGIO

Bonaventure was born in Bagnoregio, near Orvieto, in Italy. Scholars are divided on the date of his birth. The range of years goes from
1217 to 1221. His earliest education took place as a child-oblate at
the Franciscan community in Bagnoregio. As a layman, he moved
to Paris and began his studies in the faculty of arts. After he received
this degree, he joined the friars. When he began his theological studies at the University of Paris, his professors were Alexander of Hales,
William of La Rochelle, Odo Rigaldus and William of Melitona. From

1248 to 1250, he was a lecturer on the Bible. He was regent master of the Franciscan school from 1254 to 1257. In 1257, he was elected Minister General of the Friars Minor, and he remained in this position until his death in 1274. His *Commentary on the Sentences* is a major theological work of the thirteenth century, but he also published other key theological works such as: *Retracing the Arts to Theology, The Itinerary of the Mind to God, Disputed Questions on the Mystery of the Trinity* and *Disputed Questions on the Knowledge of Christ*. He also wrote a *Life of St. Francis* and many other studies on Franciscan spirituality.

He was a monumental academic leader, a powerful spiritual writer, and a major administrator of the friars during the term of his generalate. In 1273, he became Cardinal Archbishop of Albano and was entrusted with many items for the Council of Lyons. He died on July 15, 1274, while assisting at this council. Pope Sixtus IV canonized him in 1482, and, in 1588, Pope Sixtus V named him a Doctor of the Church with the title "Seraphic Doctor." Together with John Duns Scotus, Bonaventure is considered a key academic theologian of the Franciscan Intellectual Tradition.

Bonaventure had many students who became well known as Franciscan theologians. Among them are Richard Rufus of Cornwall (+1260), Gilbert of Tournai (+1284), William de la Mare (+1298), John of Wales (+1302), Richard of Middleton (+1308) and perhaps his most famous student, Matthew of Aquasparta (+1308). His influence in theological thought was strong during his lifetime and has continued to be a major factor for both Roman Catholic and Protestant theologians down to the present time.

THE FRANCISCAN SCHOOL
AT THE UNIVERSITY OF OXFORD

ROBERT GROSSETESTE

Robert Grosseteste was a diocesan priest and, for a short time, Chancellor at the University of Oxford. No one knows exactly where he studied or received his degree. In 1229, he became regent master at the Franciscan house of studies in Oxford and taught the early Franciscans until 1235. He felt very close to the Franciscan ideals and his teaching united Franciscan spirituality with theology. Many of his friends thought he would become a Franciscan, since he had taken a private vow of poverty. In 1235, he was consecrated Bishop of Lincoln. As bishop, he continued his friendship with the friars, especially his student and dear friend, Adam Marsh. Over the next seventeen years, three secular priests succeeded him as regent master of the Franciscan school. He died in 1253. The Franciscan Intellectual Tradition is deeply indebted to this diocesan theologian. At Oxford, it was he who taught the first friar students, and many of his theological positions became a central part of the tradition. Alexander of Hales, also a diocesan priest, was profoundly influenced by Grosseteste and brought to the first Franciscan friars at the University of Paris theological and philosophical positions that he had learned from Grosseteste.

ADAM MARSH

Adam Marsh joined the Order in 1227 and for forty years was a good friend and colleague of the friar, Roger Bacon. Together they researched Greek writings, treatises on mathematics, and natural science. Marsh assisted Robert Grosseteste, constructing chapter divisions and titles for Grosseteste's major work, the *Hexaëmeron*, an exegesis on creation narratives in Genesis. In 1247, Marsh became the first Franciscan regent master at the University of Oxford. He remained active until his death in 1258.

THOMAS of YORK

Thomas of York most probably was a student of Alexander of Hales. In 1253, he became the second Franciscan to be regent master at the Franciscan school in Oxford, succeeding Adam Marsh. By 1259 he had almost finished his major work, *Sapientiale*, in which he demonstrates the depth of his knowledge regarding Maimonides, Avicenna, Averroës, Aristotle and Plato. It is a "classic" in early Oxford academia. In 1256, he succeeded William of Melitona as regent of the Franciscan school in Cambridge. He died in 1260. From his youth he was a brilliant scholar. However, in spite of his brilliance, his professors at Oxford delayed his reception of the master's degree because of his youth.

RICHARD RUFUS of CORNWALL

Richard Rufus entered the Franciscans at Paris in 1238. He studied at Oxford and was the second Oxford professor and the first Franciscan professor to write a commentary on the *Sentences* of Peter Lombard. This embroiled him in a debate on the question of theology—is theology in Scripture or is it in Lombard? He died sometime after 1259.

JOHN PECHAM

John Pecham (1225-1292) was a disciple of Bonaventure at the University of Paris around 1270. He moved to Oxford in 1271 where he completed his studies in 1275. In 1279, he became Archbishop of Canterbury. On many theological issues he was conservative, mainly as regards philosophical issues that went against the Augustinian framework of his thought. For Pecham, Averroës was a pernicious heretic. He followed Bonaventure's position that God's existence is a truth that we know with immediate evidence. He stressed the superiority of the will over the intellect.

ROGER BACON

Roger Bacon was born between 1210 and 1215. He studied in the faculty of arts at the University of Oxford, focusing on Seneca and Cicero. It seems he then went to Paris and, in 1240, received his master's degree. He lectured there on Aristotle until 1246. In 1247 he entered the Franciscan Order and returned to Oxford, where he was in contact with Robert Grosseteste and Adam Marsh. His interest in science was extremely strong and his knowledge in this area was immense, given the time in which he lived. From 1266 to 1268 he composed his most important work, *Opus Maius*, an encyclopedia of the various branches of knowledge; but he also found time to compose his *Opus Minus* and *Opus Tertium*. Evidently, he was a difficult person to live with. He wrote that Richard of Cornwall was "an absolute fool," Alexander of Hales was "ignorant of natural philosophy and metaphysics" and Thomas Aquinas was full of "puerile vanity and voluminous superfluity." Such demeaning remarks seem to have been one of the major reasons for his condemnation and confinement in the Paris friary from 1277 to 1292. He died in 1292, the same year he was released from confinement.

WILLIAM of WARE

William of Ware studied at the Universities of Paris and Oxford and, from 1290 to 1300, taught as a magister in both places. He was a great friend of Roger Bacon and a follower of Bonaventure. It seems he was one of the main teachers of John Duns Scotus. He died in 1300.

ROGER MARSTON

Roger Marston studied at the University of Paris (1269-1272) and then began teaching, first at Oxford and then at Cambridge. From 1292 to 1298, he was the provincial of the English Franciscan Province. In his theology, he followed Bonaventure and John Pecham. For him, Augustine and Anselm were key theologians. Roger Marston is an example of an Augustinian-Bonaventurian theologian within the Franciscan Intellectual Tradition. He died in 1303.

JOHN DUNS SCOTUS

John Duns Scotus was born in Scotland around 1266 and died in Cologne in 1308. His uncle was a Franciscan and perhaps influenced his nephew to join the Order. Scotus studied at the University of Oxford and at the University of Paris, and he taught at the Universities of Oxford, Paris and Cologne. Aspects of his philosophy and theology will be touched on later in this volume. Bonaventure and Scotus can be considered the two main founders of the Franciscan Intellectual Tradition.

PETER AUREOLI

Peter Aureoli was born in Aquitaine around 1280. In 1304, he began his theological studies at the University of Paris and, at that time, came into contact with John Duns Scotus. He taught as a lecturer at the Franciscan house of studies in Bologna and Toulouse. In 1316 he returned to Paris and obtained a bachelor's degree and a doctorate in theology. In 1320/21, he became provincial of the Aquitaine province. In 1321, he became the bishop of Aix. He died in 1322. R. Dreiling notes that he is "not a platonist, nor an augustinian, nor an aristotelian, nor an averroist, nor a scotist, nor a thomist." He was a very independent thinker and an eclectic individual. He praises and criticizes all of the above-mentioned authors. He strongly backed the Franciscan position on individuality and on the freedom of God, which is bound by no law.

FRANCIS of MEYRONNES

Francis of Meyronnes was provincial of the Meyronnes province. He had studied at the University of Paris and was a strong follower of John Duns Scotus. Though he wrote a commentary on the *Sentences* of Peter Lombard, he was philosophically inclined. He noted that Aristotle was optimistic in physics and pessimistic in metaphysics. His works include: *On the Univocity of Being, On the First Principle, On Relations* and *On Transcendentals*. All of these indicate his connection to Scotus. In his *Commentary,* Francis of Meyronnes states that it is the earth that is moving, while the heavens remain unmoved. He died circa 1328.

WILLIAM of OCKHAM

William was born in the English village of Ockham around 1285 and died in Munich in 1347. He entered the Franciscans and began his studies at the University of Oxford, completing them around 1320. At Oxford he lectured on the *Sentences,* and his *Commentary on the Sentences* remains his most important book. Although he completed his theological studies, he was never appointed regent master of the Franciscan school. In 1323/4, John XXII summoned him to Avignon to explain fifty-six of his positions that had been criticized by the chancellor at Oxford, John Lutterell. William, a follower of John Duns Scotus, was a brilliant philosopher and a major theologian. The pope never condemned any of his philosophical or theological positions, all of which were composed before his call to the Avignon papal palace. However, some of his political positions were condemned. William fled Avignon and sought refuge from Emperor Louis of Bavaria. He remained in Bavaria until his death. Ockham's famous axiom, or as it is called "Ockham's razor," has been quoted down to our own time—beings should not be multiplied without necessity. He is also known as the founder of a Franciscan Nominalist School. Nominalism is a philosophical theory that denies the existence of universal concepts and principles apart from the human mind. Emphasis is on the individual. With no universal moral norms, morality simply conforms to a God with absolute freedom.

Francis of Assisi died in 1226. Within one hundred years of his death, we find that the theological world was richly blessed with Franciscan theologians of very high quality.

The Dominican Order also blessed the world with a large number of excellent theologians. C. H. Lawrence, in his book, *The Friars*, has a lengthy chapter entitled "The Capture of the Schools." In this chapter, he traces the first attendance by Dominicans and Franciscans at the Universities of Paris and Oxford. It was these two groups who, in Lawrence's terms, "captured the schools." He writes:

> Compared with the schools of the seculars, the system of the Mendicants had important advantages besides those of superior organization. In the secular schools men taught for a few years and moved on. University teaching was not regarded as a career for life. The pressing need to acquire a benefice, to repay debts to patrons, the expectation of a career in the higher echelons of the Church or state, constantly drew men away from the schools in early middle-life. But when a man became a friar, he opted out of the race for preferment. At the schools, freed from the pressures of secular ambitions and the struggle for livelihood, he was able to pursue scholarship with a sense of detachment. . . . If he was successful, he might be allowed to spend his whole life in the scholastic world.[10]

With so many friars, Dominican and Franciscan, attending and teaching at the universities during the thirteenth and fourteenth centuries, the two orders were able to fashion their theological traditions in an abundant way. Once more, let me say that theology and philosophy cannot be equated with the Word of God, the tradition of the Church, nor with the solemn teachings of the Church. Faith is basic. Philosophy and theology are only ways to express and understand more deeply what our faith is and what it implies. Different philosophical and theological traditions have existed in the Church from its very beginning. Intellectual traditions have helped one another and have been in conflict with one another. This is the structure of all sciences, arts, philosophies and theologies. One intellectual tradition might keep the rest honest, and the others might keep simply one of the intellectual traditions honest. It is in this arena that differences should be discussed and judged.

III. Franciscans in the Twelfth and Thirteenth Centuries Whose Careers Were Not Generally Associated with the Universities of Paris and Oxford

The listing of these Franciscan theologians is a major factor in the understanding of the Franciscan Intellectual Tradition. Through these friar theologians, the tradition was carried to places throughout the Western world at that time. Through their teachings and writings, the Franciscan Intellectual Tradition became influential even outside university or scholastic milieux.

ANTHONY of PADUA

Anthony of Padua (1191-1231). In the Franciscan Intellectual Tradition, Anthony of Padua has always held a special place. He was the first to be given the title of teacher of theology in the Order of Friars Minor. It was Francis himself who gave him this title. He had studied theology in Coimbra, Portugal, where his professors were men who had studied in Paris under Augustinian mentors. When he was fifteen he entered the monastery of the Augustinian Canons Regular just outside of Lisbon. While he was there, the remains of the first Franciscans who had been martyred in Morocco were transferred to Coimbra, where they were celebrated in a way that so impressed the recently ordained priest, Anthony, that in 1220 he transferred to the Friars Minor. His motive was to be a martyr, and he wanted to go to North Africa, which he did but only for a short time. From North Africa, he went to Sicily and then to Assisi. He taught the friars in their study houses at Montpellier and Toulouse. From 1229 to 1231, he was in Padua as a lector for Franciscan students. He died in 1231. His funeral was a major event, and only eleven months after his death, he was canonized by Pope Gregory IX. In 1946, Pope Pius XII declared Anthony a Doctor of the Church, with the title *Doctor Evangelicus*. The only written work of Anthony that we have is a book of his sermons. From these sermons, scholars have provided an analysis of his theology.

PETER JOHN OLIVI

Peter John Olivi (1247/8-1298). Peter John Olivi was born at Serignan, just outside of Béziers in southern France. He became a Franciscan in 1259/60 and a few years later began his studies at the University of Paris. Although he wanted to be a master of theology at the university, he was called back to his province in the mid-1270s, where he taught as lector for the young friars at Narbonne and, perhaps, at Montpellier. An unknown friar, referred to as "Brother Ar," drew up a list of statements of Olivi that he considered untenable. This list was sent to the proper authorities. In 1283, Olivi was censured. The process leading up to this censure was long and complicated, but his teaching career lay in ruins. Nonetheless, he represents a theological position to which many theologians at that time, in one way or another, ascribed. It was a question over the basis of theology itself. Simply stated—Does theology depend on the *Sentences* of Peter Lombard and the many commentaries on this book? Or does theology rest on Scripture? Is theology a *scientia*, that is, a scientific study, or is theology an exegesis of God's Word?

Many issues entered into this thirteenth- and fourteenth-century controversy. For the Franciscans, the issue of poverty became part of the problem. The various Franciscan interpretations of the Bull of Pope Nicholas III, *Exiit qui seminat*, escalated the struggle, since papal authority itself became an issue. Olivi's biblical theology, however, was held in high esteem by some Franciscans. Olivi held certain views that he claimed to be the correct interpretation of the vision and spirituality of St. Francis. In Olivi's theology we see both the difficulties and the values of uniting spirituality and theology, an issue which continues down to the present.

RAYMOND LULL

Raymond Lull (1232-1316). Raymond Lull was born in Palma, Majorca. His early education was not very intense. In 1257, he married Blanca Picany, and two children were born of this union. If the details of the first thirty years of his life are basically unknown, the details of the remainder of his life are well known. Lull wrote an autobiography, *Vita coaetanea*, in 1311. He was known as a man of action, a mystic and a literary figure. Recent scholarship adds another dimension. He was a prolific writer. Lull's writings total 265 items. He was also an artist, and it is this visual dimension that has aroused contemporary interest. His art is seen as a key to understanding his most profound positions. Some of his deepest books are *Ars demonstrativa, Ars generalis ultima* and *Ars brevis*.

Lull could scarcely avoid extensive praise and at the same time serious condemnation. Whether he was a secular Franciscan or not is still not sure. Anthony Bonner, a contemporary scholar on Lull, leaves the door open but says very clearly: "The only thing certain is that Lull was very close to the Franciscans in thought and spirit."[11] In the history of European thought from 1316, the year of Raymond's death, down to the present, the influence of this Majorcan and Franciscan scholar has been enormous. In his travels, his writings, his lectures and his preaching, he has disseminated the vision and spirituality of the Franciscan Intellectual Movement in a way no other person has.

PART FIVE
DISTINCTIVE FEATURES OF THE FRANCISCAN INTELLECTUAL TRADITION

Since the end of the thirteenth century, as we have indicated, there has been a form of theology called "Franciscan." The first major production of the Franciscan Intellectual Tradition was the *Summa of Alexander of Hales*. One finds in this first *Summa* several key aspects of the spiritual vision of Francis of Assisi.

- The very nature of God is love, and therefore God's will and freedom are more central than God's knowledge. Love grounds the theology of Trinity, creation, incarnation and risen life.

- The humility of the incarnation and the love of the passion are issues that begin to shape the Franciscan theology of Jesus.

- Creation contains the Word of God and the Holy Scriptures contain the Word of God, but these are not two Words of God. It is the same Triune God who speaks and calls in creation and in the Scriptures.

- Spirituality and theology are put together, for theology without spirituality is empty, and spirituality without theology is a sham.

Other key issues of the Franciscan Theological Tradition also emerged in this first *Summa*, but for now let us consider how these four ideas, stemming from the spiritual vision of Francis of Assisi, became part of a distinctive theological tradition, particularly under the influence of Bonaventure and Scotus. Distinctive insights into the Catholic Faith found a resonance in people's experience; controversy helped form the parameters of the distinctive elements; institutionalization into a "school of thought" assured some stability. In looking at the emergence of this tradition we will consider its distinctive features under two headings:

I. The Triune God: a Relational God, Who is Both *Primitas* and *Fecunditas*

Under this heading we will consider a number of theological issues centered on uncreated being, namely the Triune God.

    A. The Triune God in the Vision and Spirituality of St. Francis
    B. The Triune God as Developed in the Franciscan Intellectual Tradition
       1. Bonaventure and the Triune God
       2. Scotus and the Triune God
       3. Creation: The Doctrine of Emanation
       4. Incarnation: The Place of Jesus in Creation
       5. The Absolute Freedom of God
       6. The Humility of the Incarnation

II. The Sacred Book of Creation

Under this heading we will consider a number of theological issues centered on created being.

    A. The Book of Creation in the Vision and Spirituality of St. Francis
    B. The Book of Creation as Developed in the Franciscan Intellectual Tradition
       1. Creation as a Gift of God's Freedom and Love
       2. *Haecceitas:* The Doctrine of "Thisness"
       3. Contingency and Grace

Under each of these topics, there will be two subheadings. First, we will consider *the vision and spirituality of St. Francis*. This subheading contains a brief indication of Francis's reverence for the theme. Second, we will look at *each individual theme as it is developed within the Franciscan Intellectual Tradition*. This subheading contains a brief presentation on the major ways in which Franciscan scholars have integrated each theme into the central and constitutive core of their theology. In this way, both of these subheadings will indicate and identify the central elements constituting the Franciscan Intellectual Tradition.

I. The Triune God: a Relational God, Who is Both *Primitas* and *Fecunditas*

Theologically, the Franciscan Intellectual Tradition finds its core and its foundation in the doctrine on the Triune God. The Triune God is the firstness (*primitas*) and fecundity (*fecunditas*) of all that is, including the inner being of God. Within this inner divine being, there is a firstness and fecundity that we call "Father." The Father is not only the "first" Person of the Trinity; the Father is a fruitful, effusive "first" Person. From the Father's primal fecundity come the Son and the Spirit. The Triune God can only be understood as a relational God. There is only one God, but this is an intrinsically relational one God. In the Franciscan view, there is not an isolated, transcendent, utterly other oneness at the deepest depth of divinity. Rather, there is a diffusive firstness and a primal fecundity.

A. The Triune God in the Vision and Spirituality of St. Francis

In the writings of St. Francis, we find that he used the term, God, very often, and this does not surprise us. However, Francis is never content to speak vaguely of God, as the Franciscan, Norbert Nguyên-Van-Kahnh tells us.[12] Rather, Francis again and again speaks of a Trinitarian God. It is a Trinitarian God who creates the entire world. It is a Trinitarian God who is at the center of Francis's spiritual life. When Francis calls God "Father," he usually mentions the Son and the Holy Spirit as well. The Trinity is a relational God, a God whose very being is only understood in a relational, triune way. One citation from Francis can stand as an example of many, many other citations that might also be used.

> All-powerful, most holy, Almighty and Supreme God, Holy and just Father, Lord King of heaven and earth, we thank You for Yourself, for by Your holy will and by Your only Son with the Holy Spirit You have created all things spiritual and corporal (*Earlier Rule* 23:1).[13]

There was a profound spiritual relationship between God and Francis. Francis was a "holy" man. To be holy is to be in relation to

God. The depth of this God-Francis relation can be seen in Francis's experience of God on Mt. Alverna. The Trinity is a relational understanding of God, and Francis was well aware of this. It is remarkable to note how many times the Trinitarian relational God is mentioned in the writings of Francis. Francis loved to meditate on the greatness of God seen in the wonders of the created universe. "These wonders are accomplished in common by the three Persons of the Trinity. . . . Christ is never regarded separately from the Father and the Spirit." The centrality of the Trinity is basic to the Franciscan vision and spirituality.[14]

B. The Triune God as Developed in the Franciscan Intellectual Tradition

1. Bonaventure on the Triune God

After a few observations on what theology is and what theology includes, Bonaventure begins his *Commentary on the Sentences* with a lengthy section on God. There is nothing distinctive about this way of beginning. All medieval theologians writing a commentary on the *Sentences* began with a first distinction/question on the meaning and scope of theology. They all then addressed the God question. They simply followed the text of Peter Lombard. However, Lombard himself starts immediately with *God as Trinity*, not the *One God*. Bonaventure continues Lombard's approach.

In Bonaventure's *Commentary* there is only one opening question, *Quaestio II*,[15] on the one God, which he presents in two pages. After this short statement on God as One, Bonaventure immediately moves to the Triune God. For Bonaventure, to speak of one God at any great length is not to talk about the reality of God, namely, the Trinity. Zachary Hayes is emphatic on this. He states that Bonaventure never developed an independent treatise on the One God. "The systematic treatment of the doctrine of the Trinity constitutes the whole of Bonaventure's doctrine about God."[16] Too often in theological literature on the One God, there is an over-emphasis on the One as totally other, totally transcendent and totally independent of anything else. God's oneness becomes "aloneness," a word in which etymologically "one" equals "all" ("all-one-ness").

The mystery of the Triune God, however, stresses God as essentially relationship. The oneness of God is a relational oneness. In the Franciscan Intellectual Tradition, a relational Triune God is consistently seen as the basis for God's own nature, which is love and goodness. The medieval axiom: *bonum est sui diffusivum* ("goodness is diffusive of its very self") lies at the heart of Franciscan theological discussion on God. Bonaventure explains all of God's attributes—omnipotence, omniscience, freedom, etc.—within a Trinitarian context. Hayes goes on to say that Bonaventure's Trinitarian theology has a genuine "metaphysical status," since it "involves a penetrating insight into the mystery of Being which does not negate the metaphysical doctrine of being as known to the philosophers of antiquity but constantly holds it open to correction."[17]

Thomas Aquinas moves in a different direction. In his *Summa Theologiae*, in the initial question, *Quaestio I*, he discusses theology as a science. In *Quaestio II*, he begins his theological discussion *On God—Does God Exist?* (*De Deo—An Deus Sit?*). In this lengthy section—from *Quaestio II* to *Quaestio XXVI*—his focus is on the *One God*. Only in *Quaestio XXVII* does he begin to discuss God as Triune (XXVII to XLIII). In Aquinas, the main attributes of God are presented within his discussion on the *oneness or unity of God*. A theology that begins in a lengthy way on God as One and uses the unity of God as a major framework for the attributes of God, will differ considerably from a theology which begins in a lengthy way on the Triune God and uses the Triune God as a major framework for the attributes of God. In many ways, this difference between Thomas and Bonaventure marks a major distinction between the Dominican Intellectual Tradition and the Franciscan Intellectual Tradition. For Bonaventure, his discussion on the Trinity is not simply a prelude, playing no significant role in his subsequent theological work. Hayes stresses this: "Every major theological theme is structured by Bonaventure with reference to the mystery of the Trinity."[18] Trinitarian thinking is a structural principle of Bonaventure's entire theological vision.

Bonaventure's Trinitarian theology echoes themes from the writings of Pseudo-Dionysius (late fifth or early sixth centuries C.E.) and Hugh of St. Victor (1090-1141), two very important theological sources for all the late medieval scholastic writers. Bonaventure is also richly indebted to the trinitarian thought of his Franciscan teachers at Paris, especially Alexander of Hales and Odo Rigaldus (cf. pp. 42-3), two key scholars in the early formation of the Franciscan Intellectual Tradition. Again, we see clearly how this tradition reaches deep into the history of Christian thought and then refocuses this thinking into a structure that has been called "Franciscan."

2. John Duns Scotus on the Triune God

In the *Commentary on the Sentences*, written by John Duns Scotus, usually called the *Reportatio*, one finds a similar pattern. The first section in *Distinctio secunda* is entitled *De Esse Dei et eius Unitate* (*On the Being of God and God's Unity*). Scotus begins with three lengthy questions, but the material is very different from the material in the *Summa* of St. Thomas. Throughout his career, Scotus was deeply concerned about the human ability to come to a knowledge of God. His *Treatise on God as First Principle* is his most penetrating work on this issue, and we find in this *Treatise* a strong echo of the material in this section of his *Commentary.* His very first question is not about One God, but rather about the possibility of humans coming to know anything about God. The second question focuses on infinity. Again, this fits in well with his work in the *Treatise*, since in the *Treatise* he moves in the following basic stages:

- The univocity of being, which for Scotus is the only first step possible for any theory on the manner in which humans come to know about God. He does not call univocal being "God." Rather, it is called the first principle.

- Univocal being has a distinctive and exclusive transcendentality—in itself as being, but also as one, true and good. Scotus's presentation on the relationship of being to one, true and good is unique. The opposite of one is not two or three or many. It is absolute non-being. The opposite of true is not false, but absolute non-being. The opposite of good is not bad, but again absolute non-being. Of course, the opposite of being is absolute non-being.

- Only in the third place does Scotus discuss the polar transcendentals; and the key polar transcendental is finite-infinite. At this third level, the opposite of one is another or several; the opposite of true is false; and the opposite of good is bad.

First Question:	**Can a human being come to some knowledge of God?**
Answer:	Only through univocal being and the non-polar transcendentals.

Second Question:	**Is an infinite being a possibility?**
Answer:	Yes, and our human minds can not only pose the question but also construct a faint understanding of what this infinite being might be.

Third Question:	**Can there only be one infinite being?**
Answer:	Yes, since two or more infinite beings would be a logical impossibility.

In his *Commentary*, Scotus's first question is on the human possibility to know God. The second question is on the issue of infinity. The third question is on the possibility of two infinite beings. Only after this presentation of preliminary and epistemological issues does Scotus truly face the question of God, and the question focuses on the Trinitarian and relational God. Theologically, the only God Scotus wishes to describe is a relational, Trinitarian God. At this juncture of the *Commentary*, he moves in the exact same direction as Bonaventure. Thereafter, this focus on a relational and Trinitarian God remains central to the Franciscan Intellectual Tradition.

3.   Creation and the Triune God: The Doctrine of Emanation

A theology of creation, in the Franciscan Tradition, is meaningful only on the basis of a relational Trinitarian God. In much of Catholic theology, creation is presented as a divine work *ad extra* (outside of God's own nature), while the Trinitarian relationships constitute God *ad intra* (within God's own nature). In other words, this kind of theology presents creation as the *ad extra* work of the One God. It is only the inner life of God (*ad intra*) that is Trinitarian. The activities of God outside this inner life are seen as activities of the One God or the unity of God. This is not a Franciscan view. Only a relational

Triune God offers theological meaning for the created world. In the theology of Bonaventure, there are internal "emanations," which we call Father, Son and Spirit. However, from the neo-platonic tradition, Bonaventure capitalized on the axiom: "The more a thing is prior, the more fecund it is and the more it is the principle of otherness." From this axiom he explains that "Firstness and fecundity describe God as the fountainhead of all that is."[19] The more profound the *primitas* (firstness) is, the more generous is its *fecunditas* (fecundity).

In creation itself, we experience the presence of a Triune God, not simply of a One God. Moreover, creation itself intrinsically depends on the firstness and fecundity of the Triune God. The very term "firstness" connotes "secondness, thirdness, fourthness," etc. It connotes relationship. If there is no second, there is no first. The internal emanations of God present the Father as the most primal level of divine fullness, power and fecundity. The Son, therefore, is the *Second Person* of the Trinity and the Spirit is the *Third Person* of the Trinity. Theologians consistently use "first, second and third," when they discuss the Trinity. Franciscan theologians continue to discuss creation from the context of this primal fecundity. The Triune God is a God relating to creation, and, since creation is ongoing, the Triune God does not create once only at some "moment of creation." Rather, the Trinitarian God is continually relating to creation.[20] Creation is a book in which one can read about the presence of the Trinitarian God.

4. Incarnation: The Place of Jesus in Creation

In Franciscan theology, Jesus is also presented in the context of firstness and fecundity. For Bonaventure and Scotus, to name only two Franciscans, Jesus has a firstness and fecundity in creation itself. The incarnation is not a divine after-thought, occasioned by human sin. Rather, the incarnation has a firstness that coincides with the firstness of creation. A Franciscan cannot theologically explain creation without mentioning the firstness and fecundity of Jesus. When the Spirit of God first breathed over the abyss of meaninglessness and drew forth light, the Jesus-light was present in its firstness and fecundity. The light of Genesis and the light of the world can only be seen in their unity. This is why creation itself is the beginning of the incarnation.

When we read in St. John's gospel that the "Word became flesh" (1:14), we are drawn into a relationship of Logos or God on the one hand and a human nature or flesh on the other. The incarnation is a relating of creature and divine, a union in which Jesus is truly divine and truly human, perfect in his divinity and perfect in his humanity, one in being with the Father and one in being with all human beings (Council of Chalcedon). Creation itself is also a relating of creature and divine. In the Franciscan Intellectual Tradition, these two "relatings" are intrinsically united. Creation can be called the beginning of the incarnation, since the two are inseparable.

However, the incarnation not only begins with creation. Both creation and incarnation are incomplete or unfinished without the parousia. Whatever the parousia involves, it is an integral part of the fulfillment of creation and incarnation. The resurrection of Jesus is part of the process of creation-incarnation or incarnation-creation. The resurrection life of Jesus, united as it is with our own resurrection life, is basically more than just a continuation of life after death. It is a more intense continuation of *life in relationship with God*. Being human on this earth is one way of being human. Being human in risen life is quite another way of being human. The incarnation is God entering into our way of being human, not only through a relationship to our being human on this earth, but also through a relationship to our being human in the risen life.

These three stages of finite being—creation-incarnation-risen life—are theologically united in the Franciscan Intellectual Tradition. Creation has meaning only within its fundamental connection to the primacy and fecundity of a relational God on the one hand, and within its intrinsic relation to incarnation and risen life with God on the other hand. Incarnation has meaning only within its fundamental connection to the primacy and fecundity of a relational God on the one hand, and within its intrinsic relation to creation and to risen life on the other hand. Risen life has meaning only within its fundamental connection to the primacy and fecundity of a relational God on the one hand, and within its intrinsic relation to creation and to incarnation on the other hand. The following diagram presents a visual image of this interrelationship.

**THE TRINITARIAN GOD
RELATING
TO**

CREATION,

from its beginning to its completion

INCARNATION

from its beginning with creation to its completion

RISEN LIFE WITH GOD

from Jesus' own Resurrection
to our resurrection and
to the renewed stage
of the entire created universe

5.   The Absolute Freedom of God

There is a powerful theological realism in this. As Christians, we believe that the world we live in is a created world. We also believe that Jesus is both divine and human. We also believe that in one way or another the universe, ourselves included, will share in the end-time. These are all theological "facts" of our belief. Given these revealed "facts," the Franciscan Intellectual Tradition stresses theologizing on what is, not on what might be. Could there be a creation without incarnation? Of course. God is absolutely free to will an incarnation or not. In actuality, God did will an incarnation. Could God create a world without an incarnation and without an end-time? Again, the answer is yes. The form in which God could create and the form in which an incarnation takes place do not, in the abstract, demand an end-time, a life after death, or a parousia. In actuality,

God did not do this. The world God created and in which the incarnation of the Logos is so central does have life with God after death.

The Franciscan Intellectual Tradition does not start with what God could do, but with what God has done. In the panorama of what God has done, the tradition theologizes on its intrinsic unity. The key for this intrinsic unity is, in Franciscan thought, the incarnation. The incarnation is not theologically an afterthought of God, occasioned by human sin. The incarnation has its meaning from the first moment of creation and from the parousial life with God. What God has done deserves theological study. What God might have done is left, in Franciscan thought, to the absolute freedom of God, of which we have no clear understanding except that God is free and is free absolutely.

6.   The Humility of the Incarnation

As we have seen, Francis was overwhelmed by the humility of the incarnation. This humility of the incarnation demands a reverence for all created beings, especially the most humble of these beings. When we read the writings of Francis and Clare, we find that this emphasis on the humility of the incarnation is deeply connected with the more academic theological insights into the Triune God and on firstness and fecundity, both internal to the Triune God and external to the Triune God in creation-incarnation. All of these insights lie at the very heart and core of the Franciscan vision and spirituality, since creation is God-relating-to-our-world. Creation is the beginning of the incarnation, and the incarnation means relationship—the Logos became flesh, Jesus is truly God and truly human. When we view the incarnation through the lens of its humility and in the light of our Trinitarian theology, creation itself takes on a new aspect—the immense and sacred beauty to be discovered in the "non-event," in the insignificant and in the socially rejected.

II. The Sacred Book of Creation

The Franciscan Intellectual Tradition offers a deep theological expression of Francis's vision of the universe. Bonaventure expresses this philosophical-theological stance when he writes: "This is our whole metaphysics: emanation, exemplarity, and consummation—

to be illuminated by spiritual rays and to be led to the highest reality."[21] In the process of creation, according to Bonaventure, all things
flow out from God, manifest God, and return to God. By calling this
a "metaphysical structure," Bonaventure is stating that this is precisely what creation "is" in its being. Its very being is sacramental.
In the *Breviloquium*, Bonaventure writes:

> The created world is like a book in which its Maker, the trin-
> ity, shines forth, is represented, and can be read at three lev-
> els of expression: namely, as a vestige, as an image, and as a
> similitude. The reality of the vestige is found in all creatures;
> that of the image is found only in intellectual beings or ratio-
> nal spirits; and that of the similitude is found only in those
> creatures which have become conformed to God.[22]

A. The Book of Creation in the Vision and Spirituality of St. Francis

Throughout the writings of St. Francis, his love for creation appears again and again. The physical universe images God. The created abundance all around us is not simply a reminder of a gracious
God; rather, this abundance is the very house of God. God is present
in this abundant world, and God is sheltered in this same abundant
world. Clearly, one of the deepest expressions of God's presence in
the world is Francis's *Canticle of the Creatures*. Already in the first
two stanzas, Francis tells us that God is the ultimate desire of our
being:

> Most High, all powerful, all good Lord, all praise is yours,
> all glory, all honor and all blessing. To you alone, O Lord, do
> they belong (*Canticle of the Creatures* 1-2).

However, the second stanza clearly states that we have no direct
way to praise, honor and bless God: "No mortal lips are worthy to
pronounce your name."[23] It is in, through and with all of creation
that we are able to praise and bless God. The presence of God in all
of creation is the way in which every person, including Francis, can
reach God. Nor can it be said that Francis calls us to praise God only
"through" Brother Sun, Sister Moon, etc. Rather, he calls us to see
that Brother Sun just by being sun praises God, and Sister Moon just

by being moon praises God. Francis contemplated in creatures the wisdom, power and goodness of God. For Francis, all created things worship God, just as all human beings worship God. This was central to his spirituality.

B. The Book of Creation as developed in the Franciscan Intellectual Tradition

1. Creation as Gift of God's Freedom and Love

All mediaeval theologians understood creation as an act that only God could perform. Creation meant bringing something into being from absolute nothing. The power over finite being and absolute nothing belongs to God alone. We saw the importance of this insight when we discussed the philosophy of Aristotle. Often, however, the emphasis is on power—God has the power to create out of nothing. The Franciscan Intellectual Tradition does not start with God's power. Rather, it starts with God's absolute freedom.

In many ways, John Duns Scotus's theology of God's absolute freedom is fuller and more profound than any similar theology found in other Franciscan medieval scholars. In his *De Primo Principio: A Treatise on God as First Principle*, Scotus carefully speaks of God after a lengthy presentation on the First Principle. This comes when he treats the polar transcendentals and, in particular, the transcendental polarity of "finite-infinite." Richard Cross claims that Scotus makes infinity central to his understanding of God:

> Scotus uses the idea of divine infinity to demonstrate divine unicity and simplicity. His procedure is thus the opposite to that of Aquinas, who takes divine simplicity as basic, and thence infers infinity and unicity. Scotus expressly rejects Aquinas' attempt to derive divine infinity from divine simplicity.[24]

Infinity is basically a negative word meaning *not* finite. When one asks Scotus what is without limit in God, he is very clear. From a philosophical point of view, it is God's freedom that has no limit; and from a theological point of view, it is God's love that has no limit. There is a clear connection between God's absolute freedom and God's love. A divine act of freedom is a divine act of love; a divine act of love is a divine act of freedom.

This position of Scotus exercises an enormous role in the Franciscan Intellectual Tradition. Every single aspect of the created universe exists because of God's absolute freedom and because of God's unlimited love. All of creation is a gift. Nothing in creation is necessary. Everything, in this sense, is grace, an unmerited gift of God. Francis and Clare felt themselves surrounded by gifts. In the *Testament* Francis states:

> The Lord *gave* me, Brother Francis, thus to begin doing penance in this way: for when I was in sin, it seemed too bitter for me to see lepers. And the Lord Himself led me among them and I showed mercy to them. And when I left them, what had seemed bitter to me was turned into sweetness (*Testament* 1-3, emphasis added).

Francis of Assisi kissed the lepers and washed their wounds. This was the way God gifted him, and this gift bore the stamp of the humility of the incarnation. In this same *Testament*, Francis writes:

> Afterwards the Lord *gave* me, and *gives* me still, such faith in priests who live according to the rite of the holy Roman Church because of their orders that, were they to persecute me, I would still want to have recourse to them (*Testament* 6, emphasis added).

This gift of faith included priests who were impoverished and priests who were sinful, which indicates once more the humility of the incarnation.

Francis goes on to say that it was the Lord who *gave* him brothers, who *gave* him the ability to speak and write the Franciscan Rule. When we have an understanding that everything is gift, given by a loving and absolutely free God, then, and then only, do we begin to understand the profound meaning of creation and therefore the reverence due to creation. It is precisely in this vision of creation as gift that we see the validity and need for an ecological theology. A book by Leonardo Boff has a very important title: *Cry of the Earth, Cry of the Poor*.[25] The contents of this book are based on the reverence everyone should *give* to all people, including the poor, and *give* to all nature, for nature itself is God's *gift* to us. Reverence for nature guarantees that all, including the poor, have what they need, so all can be warm, have housing, have jobs and enjoy beauty. The exploitation of nature continues the very tears of the poor. Because all is gift, Franciscans consider the cry of the poor and cry of the earth to be a single cry.

2. *Haecceitas:* The Doctrine of "Thisness"

There is, however, a still deeper dimension of creation in the Franciscan Intellectual Tradition. In this also, Scotus is a leader. Again and again, in his writings, he treats of individuation. He coins a special term for this dimension, calling it "Thisness" (in Latin, *Haecceitas*). If one were to ask Aristotle, Thomas Aquinas and others for a definition of a human being, the answer would be immediate: a human being is a rational animal. The difficulty in this view is that God has clearly created individual rational animals, but has never created a single rational animal. One finds the meaning of rational animal only in a singular individual. Perhaps, Allan Wolter has described it best:

> Scotus's doctrine of haecceity applied to the human person would seem to invest each with a unique value as one singularly wanted and loved by God, quite apart from any trait that person shares with others or any contribution he or she might make to society. One could even say, haecceity is our personal gift from God.[26]

3. Contingency and Grace

The Triune God's freedom and love penetrate creation in yet another way; and once again Scotus has written on this in a deeper way than other scholars of the Franciscan Intellectual Tradition. This dimension is called "contingency." All creatures throughout their own particular history (as well as all of creation in its totality) depend on the firstness and fecundity of the Triune God. This means, for Scotus, that created, finite and temporal beings are so contingent metaphysically that their very essence and existence require the firstness and fecundity of the relational Triune God. If one were to take away the presence of this divine firstness and fecundity, there would be absolutely nothing, a total annihilation.

Aristotle had taught that an existent thing can be considered necessary as long as it is in existence. Most medieval theologians accepted this philosophical view. If something exists, then as long as it exists it is necessarily in existence. They argued that once God had created some being, then this being had an actual position in time and space that even God could not change. In other words, an existing creature, existing in a particular space-time, can never be said not to have existed in such a space-time. God cannot "undo" what God has "done." It is in this aspect, and only in this aspect of created things, that theologians considered a finite, temporal being necessary. This necessity is very relative. The relativity lies in its relation to the Triune God but also it is a necessity that exists only as long as a particular being exists.

Scotus, however, taught that even when a finite, temporal being is in existence, God is still absolutely free vis-à-vis that existing creature. If God remains absolutely free, then nothing outside of God can be called "necessary."

Contingency makes us look at our world in a very different way. Nothing in our universe has any necessity. Everything, therefore, is relative or "non-necessary." The incarnation, then, is not necessary insofar as it involves anything created such as the humanity of Jesus. The Church and the Church's structures are not necessary. Governments are not necessary. When one speaks of "immutable truths," one should think twice. No creature has a necessary claim on immutability.

Rather than shaking the foundations of our faith, contingency calls us back to the Triune God. *Primitas* and *fecunditas* in God are necessary; freedom and love in the Triune God are necessarily infinite. It is in the Triune God that we find the depth of necessity and the depth of freedom. In light of the Triune God, all beings are radically contingent. Where does this take us? It takes us back to seeing creation, in all its forms, as gift, as unmerited grace, as radical giftedness. Only with such a view can we catch some glimpse of the height and depth, the breadth and length of the mystery we call the Triune God. How unending is God's *primitas*, how generous is God's *fecunditas*!

PART SIX
CONCLUSION

This first volume of our series has attempted to identify some central components of the Franciscan Intellectual Tradition. From our consideration, we can conclude that this intellectual tradition has deep roots that go back to the beginnings of Christian theology. The central components have been, in one form or another, present in the spiritual depths of the Church since these same beginnings. It was the genius of the early twelfth- and thirteenth-century Franciscan theologians to gather these components into a system. They did so in a distinctly "Franciscan" format, which united the spiritual vision of Francis and Clare to a comprehensive theological vision. Thus, the tradition clearly is a spiritual-theological vision. One appreciates the theological aspect only in and through and with the spiritual aspect, and one deepens the spiritual aspect in and through and with the intellectual aspect.

Prayer is certainly more than "thinking." Prayer is an acknowledgement of God's presence that involves awe, humility, wanting more and loving what one understands of this divine presence. Prayer captures the human will and lures it further into the loving presence of God. The centrality of the will dominates the Franciscan Intellectual Tradition, and this dominance is clarified when one experiences the loving and relational presence of God as revealed to us in the Book of Creation and in the Book of Holy Scripture. The key to understanding these two books is not simply hearing but, more importantly, experiencing the Word so deeply present in the words of both books. The Incarnate Word in Franciscan spirituality and in the Franciscan Intellectual Tradition can be seen, heard, tasted and experienced only when this incarnation is seen, heard, tasted to its depth as "the humility of the incarnation" and the "love of the passion." Franciscan vernacular theology and Franciscan academic theology are intrinsically linked. They form, in all its depth and breadth, the major theological themes of the Franciscan Intellectual Tradition.

ISSUES FOR DISCUSSION

- In a group setting, explore how the notion of relationship provides a profound insight into the mystery of the Trinity and how understanding God as relational provides a profound insight into the very existence of creation. Trinity means relationship, and the universe as understood today by contemporary science is an unbelievably inter-related structure. A human life is a relational life, not only with members of a family, but with many other peoples and with physical factors and systems. Although Aristotle called relationship the least of all being, in the Franciscan Intellectual Tradition, relationship is continually center stage. How can we make the issue of relationship clearer and more effective in our Franciscan life and in our Franciscan spirituality?

- In a group setting, explore the implications of affirming the centrality of Christ in God's creative activity. This theological view has much to offer today when we are involved in ecumenical discussions among Christian groups and when we are involved in inter-religious dialogues. Inculturation, even as it occurs in our Franciscan residences and ministerial situations, is also influenced by our belief in the centrality of Christ in all creation, including all cultures.

- In a group setting, consider the Franciscan Intellectual Tradition in which sin—even "original sin"—is not central to the doctrines of creation, incarnation and risen life. The clear emphasis on grace rather than on sin challenges a number of spiritualities that are popular in the Church. Have we Franciscans taken this position seriously as far as our own spirituality is concerned?

• In a group setting, consider the implications of "Thisness" (*Haecceitas*). In the Franciscan Intellectual Tradition, this is clearly a unique element. The relationship of "Thisness" to the life and spirituality of Francis and Clare is profound. In community life and in our ministries, how can we allow "Thisness" to be far more evident, far more enriching and far more a part of our spirituality?

ENDNOTES

[1]The following material in these paragraphs is based on Michael W. Blastic, OFMConv., "It Pleases Me that You Should Teach Sacred Theology; Franciscans Doing Theology," *Franciscan Studies*, 55 (1998): 1-25, and on Zachary Hayes, OFM, "Franciscan Tradition as a Wisdom Tradition," *Spirit and Life*, 7 (New York: Holy Name Province, O.F.M., 1997): 27-40.

[2]Éphrem Longpré, "Frères mineurs," *Dictionnaire de spiritualité*, Vol. 5 (Paris: Beauchesne, 1964), 1271. Cf. the entire section 1268-1303, especially 1277-1279. For a more general treatment of theological themes in Francis of Assisi, see Thaddée Matura, OFM, *Francis of Assisi: The Message in His Writings* (St. Bonaventure, NY: The Franciscan Institute, 1997).

[3]Thomas of Celano, *The Life of St. Francis*, in *Francis of Assisi: The Saint*, ed. Regis J. Armstrong, OFMCap., J. A. Wayne Hellmann, OFMConv., William J. Short, OFM (New York: New City Press, 1999), 254. All further citations from Celano are from this same source.

[4]*Francis of Assisi: The Saint*, 177. Emphasis added.

[5]*Francis of Assisi: The Saint*, 177.

[6]Cf. Arnaldo Fortini, *Francis of Assisi*, trans. Helen Moak (New York: Crossroad, 1981), 106-9.

[7]Cf. Benjamin Z. Kedar, *Crusade and Mission* (Princeton, NJ: Princeton University Press, 1984), 119-31. Cf. also Fortini, 395-439.

[8]Cajetan Esser, OFM, and Engelbert Grau, OFM, *Love's Reply* (Chicago: Franciscan Herald Press, 1963), 23-4.

[9]Raymond Brown, SS, *The Gospel of John*, Anchor Bible Series, v. 29A (New York: Doubleday, 1970), 558-72.

[10]C. H. Lawrence, *The Friars* (London: Longman, 1994), 136.

[11]Anthony Bonner, *Doctor Illuminatus: a Ramón Lull Reader* (Princeton, NJ: Princeton University Press, 1985), 26.

[12]Norbert Nguyên-Van-Kanh, OFM, *The Teacher of His Heart* (St. Bonaventure, NY: The Franciscan Institute, 1994), 66.

[13]All references in this volume to the writings of Francis are from *Francis of Assisi: The Saint*.

[14]Nguyên-Van-Kanh, 87-88. Cf. also 59-78, 202-8, 224-230.

[15]All the medieval commentaries are divided into sections. These sections are called either Distinction I, Distinction II, etc., or Question I, Question II, etc. These Distinctions or Questions are then subdivided into Articles or Chapters. In his prologue, Peter Lombard did make mention of his various divisions, but later theologians placed the names, Distinction I, Distinction II, etc., into the text itself. Not every theologian did this in the same way.

[16]Zachary Hayes, OFM, "Bonaventure: Mystery of the Triune God," in Kenan Osborne, OFM, ed., *The History of Franciscan Theology* (St. Bonaventure, NY: The Franciscan Institute, 1994), 55.

[17]Hayes, "Mystery of the Triune God," 56. Hayes refers us to Bonaventure's *Itinerarium Mentis in Deum*, V, 308-12.

[18]Hayes, "Mystery of the Triune God," 56.

[19]Hayes, "Mystery of the Triune God," 56-60. Cf. also 62-72.

[20]Pantheism equates God with all the forces and laws of nature. This is not what the relational Triune God's presence in all creation means. Some theologians have used the word, "panentheism," to describe the presence of God in creation. This word comes closer to what the Franciscan Intellectual Tradition means by the Trinitarian relationship to creation, but as an "ism" word it remains too academic for a full expression of the Triune God's actual relationship to all of creation. The same is true of Paul Tillich's term, "theonomy." Neither term completely coincides with Bonaventure's term, "emanation."

[21]Bonaventure, *Collationes in Hexaemeron*, 1, 17.

[22]Bonaventure, *Breviloquium*, 2, 12. Cf. also Hayes, "Mystery of the Triune God," 76-7.

[23]In the *Early Rule*, Francis uses almost the same words: "All of us are not worthy to pronounce your name." *Francis of Assisi: The Saint*, 82. Cf. also Celano, *The Life of St. Francis*, ch. 29.

[24]Richard Cross, *Duns Scotus* (Oxford: Oxford University Press, 1999), 26.

[25]Leonardo Boff, *Cry of the Earth, Cry of the Poor* (New York: Orbis Books, 1997). Cf. also Prisco Cajes, OFM, *Anitism and Perichoresis: Towards a Filipino Christian Eco-Theology of Nature* (Quezon City, Philippines: Mersen Graphics, 2002).

[26]Allan B. Wolter, *Duns Scotus' Early Oxford Lecture on Individuation* (Santa Barbara, CA: Old Mission Santa Barbara, 1992), xxvii.